Study Guide for Evans

STRAIGHTFORWARD STATISTICS

FOR THE BEHAVIORAL SCIENCES

S. A. Hensch
University of Wisconsin Center
Marshfield/Wood County

Brooks/Cole Publishing Company
I(T)P™ An International Thomson Publishing Company

Pacific Grove • Albany • Bonn • Boston • Cincinnati • Detroit • London • Madrid • Melbourne
Mexico City • New York • Paris • San Francisco • Singapore • Tokyo • Toronto • Washington

Sponsoring Editor: Faith B. Stoddard
Production Coordinator: Dorothy Bell
Cover Design: Lisa Berman
Cover Photo: P.R. Production/Superstock, Inc.
Printing and Binding: Malloy Lithographing, Inc.

For more information, contact:

BROOKS/COLE PUBLISHING COMPANY
511 Forest Lodge Rd.
Pacific Grove, CA 93950
USA

International Thomson Publishing Europe
Berkshire House 168-173
High Holborn
London WC1V 7AA
England

Thomas Nelson Australia
102 Dodds Street
South Melbourne, 3205
Victoria, Australia

Nelson Canada
1120 Birchmount Road
Scarborough, Ontario
Canada M1K 5G4

International Thomson Editores
Campos Eliseos 385, Piso 7
Col. Polanco
11560 México D. F. México

International Thomson Publishing GmbH
Königswinterer Strasse 418
53227 Bonn
Germany

International Thomson Publishing Asia
221 Henderson Road
#05-10 Henderson Building
Singapore 0315

International Thomson Publishing Japan
Hirakawacho Kyowa Building, 3F
2-2-1 Hirakawacho
Chiyoda-ku, Tokyo 102
Japan

Printed in the United States of America

10 9 8 7 6 5 4 3 2 1

ISBN 0-534-33864-X

CONTENTS

An understanding of statistical concepts can help anyone become a more effective problem solver, and a solid background in statistics is a definite asset for anyone who works in behavioral or physical sciences. This study guide has been designed to assist you in mastering the core concepts and techniques in statistical analysis. Each chapter in the study guide is linked to the corresponding chapter in Evans' STRAIGHTFORWARD STATISTICS FOR THE BEHAVIORAL SCIENCES and, with the exception of the introductory and final chapters, each chapter has the same basic format.

(1) Each chapter in the study guide begins with a review of the new material introduced in the text. In this section new terms are defined and new formulas are presented.

(2) The second section of each study guide chapter contains a number of True/False questions that test your basic understanding of the factual material introduced in the text.

(3) The third section of each chapter contains Multiple Choice questions that focus on understanding and applying core concepts from the text.

(4) The fourth section of each chapter contains Matching Terms that test your understanding of the new terms introduced in each chapter.

(5) Finally, where appropriate, each chapter contains a series of practice problems that allow you practice basic computational skills.

Each of these aspects is important to your overall success in a statistics course. Statistics is a set of logical procedures for analyzing and understanding data that has its own vocabulary. The chapter review and matching term sections are designed to help you master this vocabulary. But, knowing the terms is only part of mastering the material. You also need to be able to translate and apply the vocabulary to real-world situations. The true/false and multiple choice questions are designed to help you master the core concepts and extend them to situations that go beyond the examples in the text. Finally, statistical analysis relies on mathematical procedures and the only way to become truly comfortable with the mathematical side of statistics is to practice, practice, practice. Whether your instructor has you using a hand calculator or a statistical software package it is important for you to become comfortable with the mechanics involved in calculations. The practice problems are designed to help you master fundamental statistical calculations and procedures. This is important because the mathematical formulas are only the tools of statistical analysis; however, it can be difficult to focus on the underlying concepts and principles when you are worried about making mechanical errors in calculations.

Chapter Review

Terminology

statistics	A set of logical procedures used to summarize data, test hypotheses, draw inferences and make predictions.
population	The entire set of people, things or events a researcher is investigating.
sample	A subset of a population; the portion of the population that the researcher actually observes and measures.
simple random sample	A sample that is selected in such a way that each member of the population has an equal chance of being selected, and each selection is independent of all other selections.
biased sample	A sample that does not accurately represent the population of interest.
variable	Any characteristic of people, objects or events that can take on different values.
values of a variable	The different states or magnitudes a characteristic can assume.
hypothesis	A predicted, systematic association between two (or more) variables.
causal relationship	A relationship in which a change in one variable contributes to or causes a change in the second variable.
predictive relationship	A relationship in which a change in one variable can be predicted from changes in the second variable, but where there is insufficient evidence to claim a causal relationship exists.
correlational research design	A class of research procedures that can be used to discover predictive relationships between variables.
experimental research design	A class of research procedures that use systematic manipulation to discover causal relationships between variables.

dependent variable	In an experimental study, the variable that is observed and measured by the researcher.
independent variable	In an experimental study, the variable that is systematically manipulated by the researcher.
random assignment	A procedure that ensures subjects in an experimental study have an equal chance of being assigned to each of the experimental conditions.
parameter-estimation design	A class of research procedures that are used to identify the degree or level of characteristics within a population.
measurement	Using a rule to convert observations to numbers.
data	The numbers that the researcher analyzes; the entire list of numbers is referred to as the *data set.*
quantitative variable	A variable measured on a numerical scale that is capable of distinguishing different amounts or quantities of the property being measured.
qualitative variable	A variable measured on a scale that can only distinguish differences in kind or category.
descriptive statistics	Procedures for describing and summarizing data derived from samples or populations.
inferential statistics	Procedures that enable a researcher to use sample data to estimate the characteristics of a population; these procedures can also be used to determine whether the relationships that exist in sample data are reliable or are due to chance fluctuations.
parameter	A numerical characteristic of a population; for each population parameter there is a corresponding sample statistic.
statistic	A numerical characteristic of a sample; for each sample statistic there is a corresponding parameter in the population from which the sample was drawn.

True/False Questions

____ 1. In order for a research study to produce reliable results it is necessary to study each and every element in the population that is being investigated.

____ 2. The primary purpose of statistics is to summarize data, test hypotheses, make predictions and draw inferences.

____ 3. Behavioral sciences are considered to be empirical sciences because the theories are developed and modified on the basis of behavioral observations.

____ 4. In behavioral research, the raw score that someone receives on a test would be classified as a variable.

____ 5. Two variables have a predictive relationship if a change in one of the variables contributes to or causes a change in the second variable.

____ 6. A correlational research design allows a researcher to discover whether one variable is directly responsible for an observed change in a second variable.

____ 7. If a researcher plans to identify the level of a characteristic in a population, he or she would most likely use a parameter-estimation research design.

____ 8. Two groups of subjects are statistically equivalent at the start of a study if they only have small chance differences between them on the dependent variable and any factors that might influence the dependent variable.

____ 9. In an experimental study the dependent variable is the variable that is systematically manipulated by the researcher.

____ 10. One principal distinction between experiments and correlational studies is that subjects are randomly assigned to treatment conditions in correlational studies, but not in experiments.

____ 11. Random selection is used to maximize the chances that a selected sample will accurately represent the essential characteristics of the population.

____ 12. A variable that could only distinguish three categories of a given characteristic (such as large, medium and small) would be a qualitative variable.

____ 13. The data that the researcher starts with, prior to completing any mathematical analyses are called statistics.

____ 14. Inferential statistics allow the researcher to use sample data to draw general conclusions about characteristics of populations.

____ 15. A statistically significant outcome indicates that similar results will probably occur in situations where conditions are similar to those in the research study.

Multiple Choice Questions

1. Which of the following is **NOT** one of the six stages in behavioral research?

   a. Interpreting the relationship.
   b. Choosing a research design.
   c. Randomly assigning participants to one of the conditions in the experiment.
   d. Formulating a research question.

2. Dr. Rademan is interested in discovering whether personality type is related to choice of major in University students. Dr. Rademan's research hypothesis is: People who are introverts will be more likely to enroll as business majors in University than will people who are extroverts. In this case, Dr. Rademan is most likely conducting

   a. correlation research.
   b. experimental research.
   c. parameter-estimation research.
   d. population research.

3. To study the effects of room temperature on aggression, researchers have some participants spend 15 minutes in a warm room while other participants spend 15 minutes in a hot room. In this study the independent variable is

   a. the participant's level of aggression at the end of the study.
   b. the temperature of the room that the participants are in.
   c. the length of time the participants spend in the room.
   d. the gender of the participants.

4. An animal researcher counts the number of times a rat presses a bar when different schedules of reinforcement are in place. The number of bar presses is the dependent variable. In this study the dependent variable is a

   a. qualitative variable.
   b. quantitative variable.
   c. categorical variable.
   d. random variable.

5. Descriptive statistics involves a set of procedures that can be used to

   a. draw inferences about characteristics in a larger population on the basis of data from a sample.
   b. determine whether the final outcome in a study is statistically significant.
   c. randomly assign participants to the different conditions of an experiment on the basis of chance.
   d. describe and summarize a data set.

Matching Terms

____ 1.	sample	a.	the variable that is systematically manipulated by the researcher
____ 2.	quantitative variable	b.	procedures for describing and summarizing data derived from samples or populations
____ 3.	predictive relationship	c.	the portion of the population that the research actually observes
____ 4.	inferential statistics	d.	a variable measured on a scale that can only distinguish differences in kind
____ 5.	descriptive statistics	e.	a change in one variable can be predicted from changes in a second variable
____ 6.	dependent variable	f.	a variable measured on a numerical scale that is capable of distinguishing different amounts of a property
____ 7.	parameter	g.	entire set of people, things or events a researcher is investigating
____ 8.	causal relationship	h.	a numerical characteristic of a sample
____ 9.	statistic	i.	research procedures that are used to identify the degree or level of characteristics within a population
____ 10.	parameter-estimation design	j.	the variable that is observed and measured by the researcher
____ 11.	qualitative variable	k.	research procedures that can be used to discover predictive relationships
____ 12.	correlational research design	l.	a numerical characteristic of a population
____ 13.	population	m.	a change in one variable contributes to or causes a change in a second variable
____ 14.	independent variable	n.	procedures that use sample data to estimate the characteristics of a population

Chapter Review

Terminology

nominal scale	A system of measuring that assigns observations to one category or another; nominal measurement allows the researcher to specify differences in kind but not differences in amount.
ordinal scale	A system of measuring that rank orders observations; ordinal measurement allows the researcher to specify relative differences.
interval scale	A system of measuring that assigns numbers based on actual differences between observations, but does not have an absolute zero point; interval measurement allows the researcher to specify quantitative differences but not does allow for ratio comparisons.
ratio scale	A system of measuring that assigns numbers based on actual differences between observations, and where there is an absolute zero point; ratio measurement allows the researcher to make ratio comparisons.
frequency distribution	A statistical table that provides a summary of the range of scores in a data set and the number of times each score occurs within the data set.
frequency	The number of times a score occurs within a data set.
relative frequency	The percent of the total data set that is accounted for by each specific score within the data set.
grouped frequency distribution	A statistical table that summarizes the data set using equal intervals of scores to group the raw data.
class interval	Each range of values in a grouped frequency distribution.
mutually exclusive	Indicates there is no overlap among the class intervals; each observation can be assigned to one, and only one, class interval.
all inclusive	Indicates the class intervals are exhaustive; for each observation there is a class interval to which the observation can be assigned.

exact limits	A value that lies precisely halfway between the stated upper limit of one interval and the stated lower limit of the next higher interval.
graph	A pictorial representation of either a distribution of data or the descriptive statistics derived from a data distribution.
X axis, abscissa	The horizontal axis on a graph; for a frequency distribution the *X* axis is used to represent the individual values or class intervals of the variable.
Y axis, ordinate	The vertical axis on a graph; for a frequency distribution the *Y* axis is used to represent the frequency or relative frequency of the variable.
histogram	One type of graph used to depict a frequency distribution for raw data measured on an ordinal, interval, or ratio scale; bars or columns of equal width are used to represent frequencies.
midpoint	The point which is halfway between the lower and upper limits of a class interval.
cumulative frequency	The number of values in a given interval plus the number of values that fall below the given interval.
cumulative relative frequency	The total percent of the data set that is accounted for at the upper limit of each class interval.
bar graph	A graph used to depict a frequency distribution for raw data measured on a nominal scale.
statistical curve	A relative frequency polygon for a large population of values.
negatively skewed	A frequency distribution in which most of the observations fall toward the high values of the measured variable.
positively skewed	A frequency distribution in which most of the observations fall toward the low values of the measured variable.
bimodal distribution	A frequency distribution which has two distinct peaks in the values of the measured variable.

Formulas

$$\text{Proportion} = \frac{\text{frequency of a score}}{\text{total number of scores}}$$

Percent = proportion • 100 (also referred to as *relative frequency*)

Range = Highest value - Lowest value

Exact range = Range + 1 *unit of measurement*

$$\text{Interval size} = \frac{\text{exact range}}{\text{number of intervals}}$$ (result is rounded up, if rounding is necessary)

Stated upper limit = stated lower limit + (interval size - 1 *unit of measurement*)

$$\text{Midpoint} = \frac{\text{upper limit} - \text{lower limit}}{2}$$

Cumulative frequency = number of values in an interval
+ number of values below the interval

$$\text{Cumulative percent} = \frac{\text{cumulative frequency}}{\text{total number of values}} \cdot 100$$

True/False Questions

____ 1. A nominal scale of measurement allows observations to be assigned to different categories.

____ 2. With an ordinal scale of measurement the differences between scores can be calculated and compared.

____ 3. All scales that have a zero point are ratio scales of measurement.

____ 4. Most statistical procedures assume that the data conform to an interval or ratio scale of measurement.

____ 5. Some variables can be measured using more than one level of measurement.

____ 6. A grouped frequency distribution can only be used if the data set is made up of whole numbers or frequency count data.

____ 7. All class intervals should be the same size in a grouped frequency distribution.

____ 8. The exact limit of a class interval lies halfway between the stated upper limit of one interval and the stated lower limit of the next higher interval.

____ 9. The vertical axis of a graph is also called the ordinate.

____ 10. Cumulative relative frequencies represent the percent of scores in a data set that fall below the midpoint of a particular class interval.

____ 11. When the bars in a graph share a common boundary it indicates that the variable was measured on a quantitative scale of measurement.

____ 12. If the variable on the horizontal axis of a graph is measured using the nominal scale, the category labels can arranged in any order.

____ 13. Frequency distributions can be used to determine the most "typical" outcome in a scientific investigation.

____ 14. The general rule for determining the exact limits of class intervals is to add or subtract half the unit of measurement used in the original raw scores.

____ 15. Generally, bar graphs are used for data measured on nominal or ordinal scales and histograms are used for data measured on interval or ratio scales.

____ 16. In a positively skewed distribution most of the data points lie at the low end of the scale.

Multiple Choice Questions

1. When a researcher collects raw data that is measured on an ordinal scale

    a. the data will have equal spacing between adjacent points, but will not have a meaningful zero point.
    b. the data will indicate which individuals have more or less of a characteristic, but not how much more or less.
    c. the data can be used to create proportions for the purpose of making comparisons.
    d. the data will only differentiate between various groups or categories.

2. Dr. Fitzpatrick is measuring reaction times with a timer that is accurate to 1/10 of a second. The final data are grouped into class intervals, starting with the interval 2.0 to 2.1 seconds. The exact lower limit of this interval would be

    a. 1.9 seconds
    b. 1.95 seconds
    c. 0.5 seconds
    d. 2.05 seconds

3. The following are all conventions used in constructing grouped frequency distributions **EXCEPT**

    a. all class intervals should be the same size or width.
    b. the set of class intervals should be all inclusive.
    c. there should always be at least 7 class intervals.
    d. the set of class intervals should be mutually exclusive.

4. If the highest score on a statistics exam was 96 and the lowest score was 59, the exact range of the distribution of scores for the exam would be

    a. 38
    b. 37.5
    c. 18.5
    d. 37

5. Which of the following properties is true of histograms?

    a. Histograms can be used to present data that was measured on a qualitative or nominal scale.
    b. The height of each bar should be equal to three-fourths of the bar width.
    c. The vertical edges of each bar originate at the stated limits for the class interval.
    d. Adjacent bars on the histogram should share a common boundary.

Matching Terms

____	1. mutually exclusive	a.	a frequency distribution in which most of the observations fall toward the low values of the measured variable
____	2. ordinal scale	b.	point halfway between the lower and upper limits of a class interval
____	3. exact limits	c.	indicates class intervals are exhaustive
____	4. *Y* axis, ordinate	d.	value halfway between the stated upper limit of one interval and the stated lower limit of the next interval
____	5. histogram	e.	vertical axis on a graph
____	6. ratio scale	f.	a system of measurement where there is an absolute zero point
____	7. negatively skewed	g.	frequency distribution graph for data measured on a nominal scale
____	8. nominal scale	h.	a system of measurement that assigns observations to one category or another
____	9. relative frequency	i.	frequency distribution graph for data measured on an ordinal, interval, or ratio scales
____	10. midpoint	j.	number of times a score occurs within a data set
____	11. bar graph	k.	indicates there is no overlap among the class intervals
____	12. all inclusive	l.	a frequency distribution in which most of the observations fall toward the high values of the measured variable
____	13. *X* axis, abscissa	m.	percent of the total data set accounted for by each score within the data set
____	14. frequency	n.	a system of measurement that rank orders observations
____	15. positively skewed	o.	horizontal axis on a graph

Practice Problems

1. Each of the following class intervals are selected from larger grouped frequency distribution tables. For each interval determine the midpoint and the exact lower and upper limits of the interval:

Class Interval	Midpoint of Interval	Exact Lower Limit	Exact Upper Limit
70 to 90			
10.2 to 10.8			
2 to 7			
1.50 to 1.54			
-10 to -4			
-1.0 to +1.0			

2. For the following data set you have the frequency count for each value (the total number of observations in the data set is 80). Using this information determine the relative frequency for each of the observed values.

Raw Score	Frequency	Relative Frequency
92	7	
91	9	
90	0	
89	1	
88	10	
87	20	
86	12	
85	2	
84	8	
83	11	

3. For each of the following problems you are given the values of the lowest and highest observations in a data set. Using this information determine the range and the exact range for the data set:

Lowest Value in Data Set	Highest Value in Data Set	Range	Exact Range
35	97		
2.1	5.3		
101	624		
-6	0		
5.95	11.57		
72	149		
8.4	11.0		

4. For the following data set you have the frequency count for each class interval (the total number of observations in the data set is 120). Using this information determine the relative cumulative frequency for each value.

Raw Score	Frequency	Relative Cumulative Frequency
115-119	25	
110-114	19	
105-109	14	
100-104	10	
95-99	0	
90-94	8	
85-89	5	
80-84	1	
75-79	18	
70-74	20	

Chapter Review

Terminology

central tendency	The tendency of scores to cluster around some value in a distribution of scores.
measure of central tendency	The particular value that is used to characterize a distribution's central tendency.
mode	The most frequently occurring value in a distribution of raw scores.
median	The middle score in a distribution of raw scores; 50% of the values lie above the median and 50% lie below the median (also referred to as the *50th percentile*)
N	The total number of scores or observations in a data set.
mean	The arithmetic average of a set of values; notation for a sample mean is $\overline{X}$, notation for a population mean is μ.
deviation score	The result produced when the mean for a data set is subtracted from a raw score in that data set.
least squares principle	The sum of the squared deviations from the mean of a data set will always be less than the sum of the squared deviations from any other value in the data set.
line graph	A graph in which the *Y* axis (ordinate) represents the dependent variable and the *X* axis (abscissa) represents the different levels of the independent variable.
unbiased estimator	A sample statistic whose long run, expected value is exactly equal to the value of the corresponding population parameter.
variation	The degree to which the values in a distribution tend to depart from the distribution's average value; also referred to as *dispersion.*

range	The difference between the highest and lowest scores in a distribution.
interquartile range	The range of values that includes the middle 50% of the distribution of scores; the value is derived by calculating the difference between the raw scores that fall at the 75th and 25th percentiles of the data set.
semi-interquartile range	One-half the interquartile range.
sum of squares	The sum of the squared deviations from the mean.
sample variance	The value derived by dividing the sum of squares for the sample by the total number of observations in the sample; notation is S^2.
population variance	The parameter that corresponds to the sample variance; notation is σ^2.
standard deviation	The square root of the variance; notation for a sample is S, notation for a population is σ.

Formulas

<u>Measures of Central Tendency</u>

Mode = the most frequently occurring score or observation in a data set.

$$\text{Median rank} = \frac{N+1}{2}$$

The median rank is used to locate the raw score that falls at the 50th percentile of a data set. In a data set with an odd number of observations the median will be the middle score in the data set; in a data set with an even number of scores the median will be the average of the two middle scores.

$$\text{Sample mean} = \overline{X} = \frac{\Sigma X}{N}\text{ ; Population mean (for finite populations)} = \mu = \frac{\Sigma X}{N}$$

<u>Measures of Dispersion</u>

Range = X_{max} - X_{min}

Interquartile Range = Q_3 - Q_1, where Q_3 is the 75th percentile and Q_1 is the 25th percentile.

Semi-interquartile range = $\frac{Q_3 - Q_1}{2}$

Sum of Squares = $SS = \Sigma(X - \bar{X})^2$ [Definitional formula]

Sum of Squares = $SS = \Sigma X^2 - \frac{(\Sigma X)^2}{N}$ [Computational formula]

Sample variance = $S^2 = \frac{\Sigma(X - \bar{X})^2}{N}$ [Definitional formula]

Sample variance = $S^2 = \frac{\Sigma X^2 - \frac{(\Sigma X)^2}{N}}{N}$ [Computational formula]

Population variance (for finite populations) = $\sigma^2 = \frac{\Sigma(X - \mu)^2}{N}$

Sample standard deviation = $S = \sqrt{S^2}$

Population standard deviation = $\sigma = \sqrt{\sigma^2}$

True/False Questions

____ 1. The median represents the most frequently occurring value in a data set.

____ 2. A median is only valid as a measure of central tendency if there are an odd number of observations in the data set.

____ 3. Unless a distribution is perfectly symmetrical, the sum of the squared deviations from the mode will always be greater than the sum of the squared deviations from the mean.

____ 4. In a positively skewed, unimodal distribution, the value of mean will be greater than the value of the median.

____ 5. For data measured on a nominal scale the median is the most meaningful measure of central tendency.

____ 6. When a distribution is severely skewed, the median is usually better than the mean as an index of central tendency.

____ 7. There is no valid mean that can be calculated for data measured on a nominal or ordinal scale.

____ 8. If two samples are the same size and have the same mean and median, they will also have the same range.

____ 9. For data measured on an ordinal scale either the interquartile or semi-interquartile range would be the most meaningful measure of dispersion.

____ 10. The greater the variation among the values in a distribution, the smaller the semi-interquartile range will be.

____ 11. The interquartile and semi-interquartile ranges are considered more stable measures than the simple range.

____ 12. The deviation scores should always sum to a positive number.

____ 13. The squared deviation scores should always sum to a positive number.

____ 14. The sample standard deviation represents the standard or typical amount of variation between the raw scores of a data set and the mean for the data set.

____ 15. The variance is the statistic of choice when a researcher wants a measure of variation to be in the same units as the raw data.

____ 16. The most accurate measure of dispersion for nominal data is the population standard deviation.

Multiple Choice Questions

1. The median score in a data set is

    a. the score or observation that occurs the most frequently.
    b. the score located at the 50th percentile.
    c. the measure of central tendency that is most affected by extreme scores in a data set.
    d. calculated by adding all the scores together and dividing by the total number of scores in the data set.

2. A film distributor asks patrons at a movie opening to fill in cards rating the show they have just seen. The movie patrons use a 9-point scale where 1 corresponds to "absolutely terrible" and 9 corresponds to "absolutely terrific." The first ten patrons gave the following ratings: 9, 1, 3, 8, 1, 9, 8, 2, 7, 1. What is the median rating for these ten patrons?

    a. 1.0
    b. 5.0
    c. 3.5
    d. 4.9

3. The semi-interquartile range for a data set

    a. is a measure that includes approximately 25% of the scores.
    b. measures the difference between the scores at the first and third quartiles.
    c. measures the difference between the mean and the highest score in the data set.
    d. represents the average or typical deviation between the raw scores in the data set and the mean for the data set.

4. When a researcher is working with data measured on a nominal scale

    a. the preferred measure of spread to calculate would be the population variance.
    b. measures of spread cannot be meaningfully calculated.
    c. the preferred measure of spread to calculate would be the simple range.
    d. the preferred measure of spread to calculate would be the sample standard deviation.

5. Dr. Post asks a group of parents to report the age at which their child said his or her first two-word sentence. Once the data have been collected Dr. Post determines that the mean age at which children spoke their first two-word sentence was 18.5 months, but the median age was 17.5 months and the mode was 16 months. Based on this information which type of skew does Dr. Post's data set have?

    a. The data set has a positive skew.
    b. The data set has no skew; it is symmetrical.
    c. The data set has a negative skew.
    d. The type of skew cannot be determined without more information.

Matching Terms

____	1.	sum of squares	a.	notation for the population standard deviation
____	2.	unbiased estimator	b.	value derived by dividing the sum of squares for the sample by the total number of observations in the sample
____	3.	S^2	c.	square root of the variance
____	4.	interquartile range	d.	notation indicating the values that follow should be summed together
____	5.	Σ	e.	sum of the squared deviations from the mean
____	6.	mean	f.	the most frequently occurring value in a distribution of raw scores
____	7.	deviation score	g.	notation for the sample variance
____	8.	$\overline{X}$	h.	the middle score in a distribution of raw scores
____	9.	mode	i.	range of values that includes the middle 50% of the distribution of scores
____	10.	standard deviation	j.	notation for the population mean
____	11.	μ	k.	result when the mean for a data set is subtracted from a raw score in that data set
____	12.	median	l.	sample statistic whose expected value is exactly equal to the value of the corresponding population parameter
____	13.	N	m.	arithmetic average of a set of values
____	14.	range	n.	notation for the sample mean
____	15.	sample variance	o.	difference between the highest and lowest scores in a distribution
____	16.	σ	p.	notation for the total number of observations in a data set

Practice Problems

1. For each of the following data sets determine the mode:

   a. 98, 37, 5, 33, 96, 67, 43, 33, 91, 33, 32, 8, 11
   b. 104, 2, 51, 31, 8, 101, 104, 19, 47
   c. 3, 4, 5, 3, 9, 8, 5, 7, 5, 2, 5, 1
   d. 10, 1, 9, 6, 4, 13, 2, 15, 24
   e. 8, 9, 39, 44, 55, 90, 19, 44, 28, 69, 44

2. For each of the following data sets determine the median:

   a. 48, 67, 1, 66, 45, 57, 96, 66, 40, 66, 63, 8, 20
   b. 28, 3, 10, 60, 8, 120, 29, 34, 97
   c. 6, 9, 1, 6, 4, 8, 1, 7, 1, 3, 1, 0
   d. 63, 9, 86, 16, 2, 96, 13, 67, 34, 40
   e. 8, 4, 64, 99, 11, 42, 14, 99, 38, 54, 99, 42

3. For each of the following data sets determine the mean:

   a. 72, 14, 8, 11, 75, 54, 31, 11, 76, 11, 19, 2, 66
   b. 63, 9, 86, 16, 2, 96, 13, 67, 34
   c. 1, 3, 8, 1, 7, 2, 8, 4, 8, 9, 8, 6
   d. 12, 0, 4, 5, 9, 26, 3, 31, 39
   e. 2, 7, 17, 33, 88, 73, 67, 33, 92, 57, 33

4. Using the following, calculate the sum of squares (*SS*), the sample variance S^2, and the sample standard deviation (*S*):

When ΣX is	and ΣX^2 is	and *N* is	*SS* will be	S^2 will be	and *S* will be
378	20622	13			
57	333	12			
449	24505	11			
386	26736	9			
129	3433	10			
502	32884	8			
96	1572	14			

Chapter Review

Terminology

relative measures	Mathematical transformations of raw scores to standard number scales.
proportion	The ratio of the number of target events to the total number of events in a set; calculated by dividing the frequency of the outcome of interest by the total number of events or observations in a data set.
measures of relative standing	Mathematical transformations that locate a raw score's rank or position in a sample or population.
percentile	A value below which a specified percent of a distribution of lies.
percentile rank	The percent of a distribution lying below a specified value.
standard score	A deviation score expressed in standard deviation units; also called a *z score*.
standard normal distribution	A normal distribution of *z* scores; in a standard normal distribution the mean is 0, the standard deviation is 1, and the segments of the curve are laid out in terms of various proportions of its total area.
T score	A raw score that has been transformed into a scaled score in a distribution where the mean is 50 and the standard deviation is 10.
continuous variable	Any variable that can be measured or expressed in infinitely smaller units, to any degree of precision.

Formulas

$$\text{Proportion} = p = \frac{\text{target events}}{\text{possible events}}; \quad \text{Percent} = p \bullet 100$$

$$\text{For a population: } z = \frac{X - \mu}{\sigma}; \text{ For a sample: } z = \frac{X - \overline{X}}{S}$$

For a population: raw score = $(\sigma \bullet z) + \mu$; For a population: raw score = $(S \bullet z) + \overline{X}$

True/False Questions

____ 1. The value for a proportion will always be between .00 and 1.00.

____ 2. An individual who scored 96% on an exam would have a percentile rank of 96 for that exam.

____ 3. Approximately 95% of a normal distribution lies between -2σ and $+2\sigma$.

____ 4. A value that converts to a negative *z* score will be less than the mean for the data set.

____ 5. Converting a skewed distribution of raw scores to *z* scores will change the shape of the distribution to a standard normal curve.

____ 6. The mean of a distribution of *z* scores is always 0 and the standard deviation of the distribution is always 1.

____ 7. 100% of the scores in a normal curve lie between -4σ and $+4\sigma$.

____ 8. When the proportion of the normal curve that lies below any given *z* score is multiplied by 100, the result is a percentile rank.

____ 9. With a highly skewed data set the most efficient way to determine the percentile rank of a given score is to convert it to a *z* score and compare the resulting *z* score to a standard normal distribution.

Multiple Choice Questions

1. Which of the following is **NOT** a true statement about the distribution of *z* scores?

   a. The standard deviation of a distribution of *z* scores will always equal one.
   b. The mean of a distribution of *z* scores will always equal zero.
   c. When raw scores are transformed to *z* scores the resulting distribution of scores is always symmetrical and bell-shaped.
   d. The variance of a distribution of *z* scores will always equal one.

2. Mary and Jack are enrolled in different sections of Biology 101; the instructor reports individual test scores using *z* scores. Mary earned a *z* score of 2.00; the class average for her section was 60, with a standard deviation of 5. Jack earned a *z* score of 1.50; the class average in his section was 67, with a standard deviation of 2. Which student earned the higher raw score on the exam?

   a. Mary earned a higher raw score than Jack.
   b. Jack earned a higher raw score than Mary.
   c. Both students earned the same raw score on the exam.
   d. It is impossible to determine without additional information.

3. Sue Ann completed an I.Q. test and learned her raw score was 55 out of 75. If the average for the I.Q. test was 50 with a standard deviation of 10, what would Sue Ann's *z* score be for the I.Q. test?

   a. +0.73
   b. +0.50
   c. +0.90
   d. -0.50

4. Robert's professor tells him that his *z* score for the final exam was +1.74, and that the scores for the final exam were normally distributed. What proportion of his class did Robert outscore?

   a. 45.91%
   b. 4.09%
   c. 95.91%
   d. 54.09%

5. What is the value of a *z* score that falls at the 20th percentile of the normal distribution?

   a. +0.53
   b. -0.84
   c. +0.84
   d. -0.53

Matching Terms

____	1. proportion	a.	mathematical transformations that locate a raw score's rank or position in a sample or population
____	2. standard score	b.	percentage of a distribution below a specified value
____	3. measures of relative standing	c.	a raw score that has been transformed into a scaled score in a distribution where the mean is 50 and the standard deviation is 10
____	4. *T* score	d.	mathematical transformations of raw scores to standard number scales
____	5. percentile rank	e.	a deviation score expressed in standard deviation units
____	6. relative measures	f.	ratio of the number of target events to the total number of events in a set

Practice Problems

1. Using the following, calculate the *z* score that corresponds to the raw score indicated:

When $\overline{X}$ is	and S is,	a raw score of	will convert to a *z* score of:
97	9.23	100	
46	8.01	38	
8	0.52	9	
22	1.37	24	
31	4.69	24	
54	7.15	39	
100	6.48	110	
75	3.74	73	

2. For each of the following, use Table Z to determine the proportion of the normal distribution contained between the *z* scores provided (note: ∞ signifies infinity):

Between $z =$	and $z =$	the proportion of the normal distribution is:
+0.57	$+\infty$	
$-\infty$	- 1.36	
-1.21	-0.46	
$-\infty$	+0.12	
-0.61	$+\infty$	
+1.85	+1.99	
-0.29	+0.97	

3. For each of the following, use Table Z in Appendix A to determine the percentile rank of the *z* score provided:

A *z* score of	has a percentile rank of:
+0.69	
-1.12	
-3.37	
+2.57	
-2.02	
+3.12	
+1.58	
-0.74	

4. Using the following, estimate the raw score that corresponds to the z score indicated:

When $\overline{X}$ is	and S is,	a z score of	will correspond to a raw score of:
28	5.17	-1.62	
69	2.35	+2.58	
7	0.86	+1.05	
41	4.73	-2.37	
72	1.07	+0.41	
85	3.21	-3.19	
150	9.61	-0.26	
36	6.59	+3.70	

Chapter Review

Terminology

Pearson *r*	A numerical index of the strength and direction of linear association between two variables; assumes the data consist of pairs of observations, and the two variables being correlated have a linear relationship.
predictor variable	The *X* variable in a correlational analysis; also referred to as the *independent variable.*
criterion variable	The *Y* variable in a correlational analysis; also referred to as the *dependent variable.*
magnitude of association	An index of the strength of the relationship between two variables; measured by the absolute value of *r* which can range from 0.00 to 1.00; the greater the absolute value of *r*, the stronger the relationship between the two variables.
negative (inverse) correlation	The type of relationship that exists when values of two variables tend to change in opposite directions; an increase in the value of one variable tends to be associated with a decrease in the value of the second variable.
positive (direct) correlation	The type of relationship that exists when values of two variables tend to change in the same direction; an increase in the value of one variable tends to be associated with an increase in the value of the second variable.
scatter diagram (scatterplot)	A graph in which the values for the criterion variable (*Y*) are plotted against the corresponding values of the predictor variable (*X*).
line of best fit	A line that passes through the middle of the plotted points in a scatter diagram; also referred to as a *regression line.*
curvilinear relationship	A situation where two variables have a strong relationship, but where the relationship is non-linear.

spurious r	A fairly large numerical correlation that is not reliable and will not be reproducible in subsequent studies of the same relationship.
proportion of variance accounted for	The proportion of variation in variable Y that can be predicted from knowing variable X.
coefficient of determination (r^2)	The proportion of variance in variable Y that is accounted for by variable X.
coefficient of nondetermination	The proportion of variance in variable Y that is **NOT** accounted for by variable X.
restriction of range	Anything that causes a decreased range of scores on variable X or variable Y ; the resulting correlation coefficient will be have a smaller value than would be the case if the range of values was not restricted.

Formulas

$$r = \frac{\Sigma(z_X \bullet z_Y)}{N}$$ [Definitional formula]

$$r = \frac{CP_{XY}}{\sqrt{SS_X \bullet SS_Y}}$$ [Computational formula]

Adjusted sum of the cross-products of X and Y = $CP_{XY} = \Sigma(XY) - \frac{(\Sigma X \bullet \Sigma Y)}{N}$

Sum of squares $X = SS_X = \Sigma X^2 - \frac{\Sigma(X)^2}{N}$

Sum of squares $Y = SS_Y = \Sigma Y^2 - \frac{(\Sigma Y)^2}{N}$

True/False Questions

____ 1. The criterion variable in a correlational analysis can also be referred to as the dependent variable.

____ 2. A high positive correlation indicates that variable *X* causes a predictable change in variable *Y*.

____ 3. The Pearson *r* can only be used with data that have a perfectly linear relationship.

____ 4. Two variables with a correlation of -0.87 have a stronger association than two variables with a correlation of +0.69.

____ 5. An inverse correlation indicates that two variables tend to change in opposite directions.

____ 6. If two variables have a low correlation, such as $r = +0.04$, the two variables cannot have a strong relationship to one another.

____ 7. A meaningful value for the Pearson *r* can be determined for any data set that contains matched pairs of observations.

____ 8. Direct relationships in a set of data are always stronger than indirect or inverse relationships in a data set.

____ 9. As a general rule, the larger the number of paired observations in a data set, the more confidence a researcher can have in the reliability of *r*.

____ 10. The proportion of variance in variable *Y* that can be accounted for by variable *X* is equal to r^2.

____ 11. A correlation of -0.60 is approximately twice as strong as a correlation of +0.30.

____ 12. Restricting the range of values for either variable *X* or variable *Y* will tend to produce a correlation coefficient that is smaller than it should be.

____ 13. A meaningful correlation coefficient can only be calculated for variables measured on interval or ratio scales.

____ 14. The absolute value of a correlation coefficient can range from 0.00 to 1.00.

____ 15. The sign of the correlation coefficient can be used to determine the strength of the relationship between two variables.

____ 16. The relative strength of the relationships in different samples is most accurately assessed by comparing the r^2 values for the samples.

Multiple Choice Questions

1. Which of the following correlation coefficients indicates the strongest relationship between the two variables being measured?

    a. +1.54
    b. 0.00
    c. -0.83
    d. +0.69

2. Dr. Barnes creates a scatterplot of two variables and finds that the points seem to follow a pattern that goes down, and to the right. Based on this information what can Dr. Barnes conclude about the relationship between the two variables?

    a. High scores on one of the variables will tend to be associated with low scores on the second variable.
    b. Low scores on one of the variables will tend to be associated with low scores on the second variable.
    c. The two variables have a positive or direct relationship with each other.
    d. The variable that has the greatest range of values is the dependent variable.

3. Dr. Hall conducts a survey of 100 college students to investigate the relationship between textbook price and ratings of textbook readability. The correlation coefficient Dr. Hall calculates is +0.66. Based on this information, what type of conclusion can Dr. Hall report?

    a. Increases in textbook price produce an increase in perceptions of readability in approximately 2/3 of college students.
    b. Students tend to rate readability more highly when book prices are high than when book prices are low.
    c. Students tend to rate readability more highly when book prices are low than when book prices are high.
    d. Increases in textbook price produce a decrease in perceptions of readability in approximately 2/3 of college students.

4. Dr. Ames has found that all students in one particular course tend to score between 75% and 80% on the final exam, no matter how they scored on the midterm exam. This suggests that

    a. Dr. Ames should change the final exam to make it more fair to students who are doing well in the course.
    b. scores on the final exam are negatively correlated with scores on the midterm.
    c. scores on the final exam have a null relationship with scores on the midterm.
    d. scores on the final exam are positively correlated with scores on the midterm.

Matching Terms

____ 1.	Pearson *r*	a.	relationship that exists when values of two variables tend to change in the same direction
____ 2.	inverse correlation	b.	the predictor variable in a correlational analysis
____ 3.	dependent variable	c.	low numerical correlation that indicates two variables do not covary
____ 4.	linear relationship	d.	proportion of variance in variable *Y* accounted for by variable *X*
____ 5.	coefficient of nondetermination	e.	two variables covary in such a way that a scatterplot of the paired values shows a strong, non-linear relationship
____ 6.	spurious *r*	f.	Any factor that causes a decrease in the variability for scores on variable *X* or variable *Y*
____ 7.	coefficient of determination	g.	the criterion variable in a correlational analysis
____ 8.	independent variable	h.	relationship that exists when values of two variables tend to change in opposite directions
____ 9.	null relationship	i.	proportion of variance in variable *Y* unaccounted for by variable *X*
____ 10.	direct correlation	j.	two variables covary in such a way that a scatterplot of the paired values produces a reasonable approximation of a straight line
____ 11.	curvilinear relationship	k.	fairly large numerical correlation that is not reliable
____ 12.	restriction of range	l.	numerical index of the strength and direction of linear association between two variables

Practice Problems

1. Using the following, calculate the value of the correlation coefficient (r):

When ΣX is,	ΣX^2 is,	ΣY is,	ΣY^2 is,	ΣXY is,	and N is,	r will be
595	42803	638	44422	36006	11	
495	32803	464	26568	18399	12	
532	38834	289	9683	16449	15	
586	42722	595	42803	31220	10	
501	33967	495	32803	1562	20	
289	9683	501	33967	11017	17	

Chapter Review

Terminology

linear regression analysis	The general procedure of using the correlation coefficient (*r*) to predict future outcomes.
z'_Y	The predicted *z* score for variable *Y*.
Y'	The predicted raw-score value of *Y*.
slope (*b*)	The number of units of change in *Y'* for each unit increase in variable *X*; also referred to as the *regression coefficient..*
Y-intercept (*a*)	The value of *Y'* when the regression line crosses the *Y* axis; the predicted value of *Y* when $X = 0$.
prediction error	The deviation between the actual *Y* value and the *Y* value predicted using the regression formula.
principle of least squares	Predictions produced by $Y' = bX + a$ will always yield the smallest possible sum of squared prediction errors.
linearity assumption	assumption that variables *X* and *Y* have a straight-line relationship.
homoscedasticity assumption	The assumption that the variation of actual *Y* scores around predicted *Y* scores is the same along the entire regression line; $S_{est.Y}$ has the same value for each and every predicted *Y* value.
bivariate normality assumption	The assumption that *Y* is normally distributed at every level of *X*.
cross-validation study	Using a regression model in a new sample to determine if the accuracy of the original predictions is maintained.
partitioning variance	Breaking the variance in variable *Y* into two parts: a proportion that is predictable from variable *X* and a proportion that is not predictable from variable *X*.
variance of prediction errors	The part of variation in *Y* that is not predictable on the basis of variable *X*; ($S^2_{pred.errors}$).

coefficient of determination (r^2) — The proportion of variance in variable Y that is accounted for by variable X.

coefficient of nondetermination (k) — The proportion of variance in variable Y that is **NOT** accounted for by variable X.

standard error of estimate ($S_{est.Y}$) — A numerical index of the average amount of deviation of Y from Y' along the regression line.

Formulas

$$z'_Y = r\, z_X$$

$$Y' = bX + a$$

$$b = r\,(S_Y / S_X)$$

$$a = \overline{Y} - b\overline{X}$$

$$S_{est.Y} = \sqrt{\frac{\sum (Y - Y')^2}{N-2}} \quad \text{[Definitional formula]}$$

$$S_{est.Y} = \left(\sqrt{S_Y^2(1-r^2)}\right)\left(\sqrt{\frac{N}{N-2}}\right) \quad \text{[Computational formula]}$$

$$S^2_{explained} = S^2_Y - S^2_{pred.errors}$$

$$r^2 = \frac{S^2_{explained}}{S^2_Y}$$

$$k = \frac{S^2_{pred.errors}}{S^2_Y}$$

True/False Questions

____ 1. One of the essential assumptions in linear regression analysis is that variables X and Y have a straight line relationship with one another.

____ 2. When $r = 0.00$, the best prediction for every X value is that $z'_Y = 1.00$.

____ 3. When $r < 1.00$, the predicted Y value will be relatively closer to $\overline{Y}$ than the corresponding X value is to $\overline{X}$.

____ 4. The slope refers to the number of units of change in Y' for each unit increase in variable X.

____ 5. The intercept is the point at which the regression line crosses the X axis.

____ 6. When calculating the slope of a regression line, the result should be reported using a maximum of two decimal places.

____ 7. Prediction errors $(Y - Y')$ may be positive or negative.

____ 8. The sum of the prediction errors will always be 0.00.

____ 9. As the correlation between variables X and Y decreases, the value of $\Sigma(Y - Y')^2$ will increase.

____ 10. The data points will be scattered further from the regression line when the prediction equation is more accurate.

____ 11. The homoscedasticity assumption will be violated if the amount of scatter among the actual Ys does not vary from one predicted Y-value to the next.

____ 12. The linearity assumption states that the actual Y values are normally distributed around the corresponding predicted Y values.

____ 13. The standard error of estimate provides an objective way of confidently stating the margin of error in the predictions based on a regression line.

____ 14. The standard deviation of prediction errors is also called the standard error of estimate.

____ 15. The variance in variable Y can be partitioned into two components: explained and unexplained variance.

____ 16. The explained variance provides an estimate of how much of the change in variable Y is caused by variable X.

____ 17. The coefficient of determination provides an estimate of the total variation in variable Y.

Multiple Choice Questions

1. Assume that you measure the relationships between a number of variables and calculate the following correlation coefficients: +0.23; -0.17; -0.88; +0.54. For which pair of variables would you expect the value of $\Sigma(Y - Y')^2$ to be the smallest?

   a. The variables with a correlation coefficient of +0.23.
   b. The variables with a correlation coefficient of +0.54.
   c. The variables with a correlation coefficient of -0.17.
   d. The variables with a correlation coefficient of -0.88.

2. Assume that a researcher finds a new predictor variable that has a higher correlation with the criterion variable he or she is predicting. When a regression line is constructed using the new predictor variable the value of $\Sigma(Y - Y')^2$ will

   a. increase.
   b. decrease.
   c. stay the same.
   d. not change in a predictable way.

3. Which of the following is **NOT** one of the major methods for assessing the precision of a regression equation?

   a. examining how well the regression equation predicts future *Y* values with a new sample of subjects.
   b. partitioning the variance in the regression equation.
   c. calculating the standard error of estimate.
   d. conducting a least squares analysis.

4. If the relationship between two variables fits the regression line $Y' = 4.12X + 13$, when a scatterplot is constructed the regression line will

   a. cross the *Y* axis at 4.12.
   b. cross the *X* axis at 4.12.
   c. cross the *Y* axis at 13.
   d. cross the *X* axis at 13.

5. In a regression line the value Y' represents

   a. the predicted value for the *Y* variable.
   b. the difference between the actual value of the *Y* variable and the value predicted by the regression line.
   c. the value the *Y* variable would have if it were perfectly correlated with the *X* variable.
   d. the actual value of the *Y* variable in the original data set.

Matching Terms

____ 1. slope

____ 2. intercept

____ 3. *X*-variable

____ 4. *Y*-variable

____ 5. *Y* '

____ 6. prediction error

____ 7. cross-validation

____ 8. linearity assumption

____ 9. homoscedasticity assumption

____ 10. bivariate normality assumption

____ 11. variance of prediction errors

____ 12. standard error of estimate

a. assumption that *Y* is normally distributed at every level of *X*

b. the predicted raw-score value of *Y*

c. the value of *Y* when the regression line crosses the *Y* axis

d. examining how well a regression equation predicts values in a new sample

e. numerical index of the average amount of deviation of *Y* from *Y*′ along the regression line

f. number of units of change in *Y*′ for each unit increase in variable *X*

g. assumption that the spread of actual *Y* scores around predicted *Y* scores is the same all along the regression line

h. the proportion of the variation in *Y* that is not predictable on the basis of variable *X*

i. deviation between the actual *Y* value that a subject has and the *Y* value predicted using the regression formula

j. predictor variable used to estimate values of a criterion variable

k. assumption that variables *X* and *Y* have a straight-line relationship

l. criterion variable whose values can be estimated using a predictor variable

Practice Problems

1. Using the following, determine how much the value of *Y* will change:

When *b* is	and *X*	*Y* will
+0.56	increases 5 units	
-2.36	increases 4 units	
+1.24	decreases 10 units	
-7.01	decreases 2 units	
+3.71	increases 1 units	
-1.69	increases 7 units	
+2.17	decreases 6 units	
-0.52	decreases 11 units	
+5.63	increases 8 units	
-0.47	increases 12 units	
+0.98	decreases 9 units	
-4.82	decreases 3 units	

2. Using the following, calculate the value for the slope of the regression line:

When S_X is	and S_Y is	and *r* is	the slope will be
2.34	17.91	+0.12	
11.59	1.43	-0.46	
5.67	4.86	+0.85	
8.47	3.72	-0.27	
7.13	12.54	+0.63	
9.26	0.69	-0.90	

3. Using the following, calculate the value for the intercept of the regression line:

When $\overline{Y}$ is	and $\overline{X}$ is	and *b* is	the intercept will be
11.61	17.22	-3.45	
27.37	1.98	+0.14	
100.87	50.03	-0.98	
0.54	4.61	+2.83	
54.19	0.87	-1.16	
72.25	49.58	+1.27	

4. Using the following, calculate the value for the standard error of estimate ($S_{est.Y}$):

When S_Y is	and r^2 is	and N is	$S_{est.Y}$ will be
1.64	+0.96	25	
7.35	+0.18	40	
2.87	+0.43	36	
3.02	+0.54	60	
10.49	+0.21	12	
5.10	+0.75	100	

Chapter Review

Terminology

simple random sampling	Samples are drawn from a larger population in such a way that every possible sample of size *N* has an equal chance of being drawn; each element in the population has an equal and independent chance of being selected for the sample.
nonrandom sample	A sample that is selected on the basis of convenience.
sampling distribution	The theoretical distribution of a sample statistic for all possible samples of a fixed size drawn from a given population.
unbiased estimator	A sample statistic whose long run, expected value is exactly equal to the value of the corresponding population parameter.
sampling distribution of $\overline{X}$	The distribution of sample means when each possible sample of size *N* is drawn from a population.
error of estimation	The absolute value of the difference between a sample statistic and the population parameter it estimates.
central limit theorem	Regardless of the distribution of the parent population, the distribution of means from random samples of fixed size *N* will approach a normal distribution (with mean μ and variance σ^2/N) as the size of the sample is increased.
standard error of the mean	The standard deviation of the sampling distribution of $\overline{X}$.
confidence factor	The *z* score that corresponds to a particular normal-curve area; the size of the *z* score determines the width of the confidence interval.
point estimation	A single value or sample statistic (such as $\overline{X}$) used to estimate a population parameter (such as μ).
sampling error	The random differences between the values of sample statistics and the values of the corresponding population parameters.

interval estimation	A range of values used to estimate a population parameter (such as μ).
confidence interval	A range of values that has a specified, long-run probability of containing the true value of the population parameter being estimated.
bound on the error of estimation	The distance between the sample statistic (such as $\overline{X}$) and the upper and lower boundaries of a confidence interval; when the population mean (μ) is being estimated, the distance will be equal to $z_c \sigma_{\overline{X}}$.

Formulas

Variance of the sampling distribution of $\overline{X} = \sigma^2_{\overline{X}} = \dfrac{\sigma^2}{N}$

Standard error of the mean $= \sigma_{\overline{X}} = \sqrt{\dfrac{\sigma^2}{N}} = \dfrac{\sigma}{\sqrt{N}}$

Confidence interval for the population mean $= \overline{X} \pm z_c \sigma_{\overline{X}}$

NOTE: The two most common values for z_c are 1.96 (95% confidence interval) and 2.58 (99% confidence interval)

Confidence interval for a proportion $= P \pm z_c \sigma_P$

$\sigma_P = \sqrt{\dfrac{pq}{N}}$; where $q = (1 - p)$

NOTE: Using $p = 0.5$ produces the widest (most conservative) interval

True/False Questions

____ 1. When larger samples are drawn from a population, the average error of estimation will decrease.

____ 2. When $N \geq 20$, the sampling distribution of the mean ($\overline{X}$) can be assumed to follow the normal distribution.

____ 3. Smaller samples tend to give more precise estimates of μ than larger samples.

____ 4. In parameter estimation, a random sample drawn from the population is used to draw a general inference about the population.

____ 5. Using a 99% confidence factor will produce a larger, less precise interval estimate than using a 95% confidence factor.

____ 6. A researcher who uses $z_c = 1.96$ to construct an interval estimate for a population mean can be 95% confident that the true population mean (μ) is within the confidence interval.

____ 7. When a researcher samples "with replacement" from a finite population, each member of the population can only be included once in the final sample.

____ 8. The shape of the sampling distribution of the mean ($\overline{X}$) will always be the same shape as the distribution for the sample data.

____ 9. The value for the standard error of the mean ($\sigma_{\overline{X}}$) will always be less than the value for the population standard deviation (σ).

____ 10. In the long run, a researcher has approximately a 50% chance of selecting a sample where the sample mean ($\overline{X}$) is within $\pm 0.67\,\sigma_{\overline{X}}$ of the population mean (μ).

____ 11. As the value of the confidence factor (z_c) increases, the size of the confidence interval will decrease and estimates will become more precise.

____ 12. Based on Table Z in Appendix A, the confidence factor for 90% confidence interval would be $z_c = 1.65$.

____ 13. On average, in 95 of every 100 simple random samples a confidence interval formed by $\overline{X} \pm 1.96\,\sigma_{\overline{X}}$ will include μ.

____ 14. In constructing a confidence interval for a population proportion, using $p = 0.50$ will produce the maximum possible value for σ_P and the widest possible confidence interval for a given confidence factor.

Multiple Choice Questions

1. Dr. Dyler uses a single statistic ($\overline{X}$) from a sample to estimate the corresponding population parameter. Dr. Dyler

   a. can be 99% certain that $\overline{X}$ accurately estimates the value for μ.
   b. is making a point estimate.
   c. will be inaccurate in his or her estimate 5% of the time.
   d. is constructing an interval estimate.

2. When population parameters are being estimated, a statistic that is unbiased

   a. will be equal to the population parameter 95% of the time.
   b. will use all the information in a given sample.
   c. requires a sample size of $N \geq 30$.
   d. will have a long run, expected value that is exactly equal to the value of the corresponding population parameter

3. Assume that the following four samples are selected. In which of the samples would the value for the standard error of the mean be the lowest?

   a. A sample of 16 drawn from a population where $\mu = 20$ and $\sigma = 10$.
   b. A sample of 4 drawn from a population where $\mu = 50$ and $\sigma = 10$.
   c. A sample of 25 drawn from a population where $\mu = 10$ and $\sigma = 20$.
   d. A sample of 9 drawn from a population where $\mu = 75$ and $\sigma = 20$.

4. Following a research study, Dr. Johnson calculates $\sigma_{\overline{X}} = 3$. If the population standard deviation for the variable being measured is equal to 15, how many people took part in Dr. Johnson's study?

   a. 25
   b. 5
   c. 125
   d. It is impossible to determine from the information provided.

5. Dr. Syring administered a reading comprehension test to 100 students. The mean score in the sample was $\overline{X} = 52$. The standard deviation for the population was known to be 10. Given this information, the 95% confidence interval for the true population mean (μ) would be

   a. 49.42 to 54.58
   b. 51.38 to 52.62
   c. 50.04 to 53.96
   d. 51.18 to 52.82

Matching Terms

____ 1.	sampling distribution	a.	standard deviation of the sampling distribution of $\overline{X}$
____ 2.	$z_c = 2.58$	b.	a sample drawn in such a way that each element in the population has an equal and independent chance of being selected
____ 3.	point estimation	c.	z score that corresponds to a particular normal-curve area
____ 4.	error of estimation	d.	95% confidence factor for interval estimation
____ 5.	confidence interval	e.	using a range of values to estimate the true value of a population parameter
____ 6.	simple random sample	f.	a range of values that has a specified, long-run probability of containing the true value of the population parameter being estimated
____ 7.	sampling error	g.	using a single value or sample statistic to estimate the value of a population parameter
____ 8.	$z_c = 1.96$	h.	distance between a sample statistic and the upper and lower boundaries of a confidence interval
____ 9.	bound on the error of estimation	i.	absolute value of the difference between a sample statistic and the population parameter it estimates
____ 10.	confidence factor	j.	random differences between the value of a sample statistic and the value of the corresponding population parameter
____ 11.	interval estimation	k.	theoretical distribution of a sample statistic for all possible samples of a fixed size drawn from a population
____ 12.	standard error of the mean	l.	99% confidence factor for interval estimation

Practice Problems

1. Using the following, calculate 95% confidence intervals for the population mean:

When $\overline{X}$ is,	σ is,	and N is,	the 95% confidence interval for μ will be:
1096	72	121	
16	4	64	
140	10	36	
50	10	81	
90	28	169	
7	2	4	

2. Using the following, calculate 99% confidence intervals for the population mean:

When $\overline{X}$ is,	σ is,	and N is,	the 99% confidence interval for μ will be:
2543	41	81	
25	8	4	
107	12	36	
48	7	49	
89	15	64	
11	3	121	

3. Using the following, calculate the most conservative 95% confidence interval for the population proportion:

When P is,	and N is,	the 95% confidence interval for the population proportion will be:
0.25	36	
0.49	81	
0.87	64	
0.50	4	
0.09	121	
0.61	49	

Chapter Review

Terminology

reliable	A research outcome that is likely to be repeated in its basic form if the same study is replicated; may also be referred to as *statistical significance.*
null hypothesis, H_0	The statistical hypothesis which states that the observed outcome is due to chance variation.
alternative hypothesis, H_1	The statistical hypothesis which states that the observed outcome is due to factors other than chance variation.
test statistic	A numerical index, computed from the sample data, which can be compared with a sampling distribution of chance statistics of the same type.
nondirectional test of significance	The type of hypothesis test used when the researcher is interested in detecting extreme values in either end of the sampling distribution.
statistically significant result	Any test statistic that has an extremely low probability of occurrence in a distribution of chance events; 5% is the most typical criterion used to assess test statistics but different probability levels may be selected by a researcher.
level of significance	The probability level a researcher selects to assess the test statistic computed from a data set; in the behavioral sciences the level of significance is typically set at 5%.
critical value	The theoretical value of a test statistic that would be required for significance; the critical value for the test statistic is determined using statistical tables.
region of rejection	The extreme portion of the sampling distribution that represents statistically significant outcomes.
two-tailed test	A nondirectional test of a research hypothesis which has a rejection region in both extremes of the sampling distribution; in general, behavioral scientists use nondirectional tests unless there is a compelling reason to restrict the region of rejection to one side of the sampling distribution.

one-tailed test	A directional test of a research hypothesis in which the entire rejection region is located in one extreme of the sampling distribution; in general, behavioral scientists do not use directional tests unless there is a compelling reason to restrict the region of rejection to one side of the sampling distribution.
Type I error	Making an incorrect decision by rejecting the null hypothesis when the null hypothesis is actually true.
Type II error	Making an incorrect decision by failing to reject the null hypothesis when the null hypothesis is actually false.
alpha level (α)	The probability of making a Type I error in a hypothesis test; the level of significance for a hypothesis test is usually referred to as the alpha level.
beta (ß)	The probability of making a Type II error in a hypothesis test.
power	The probability of correctly detecting and rejecting a false null hypothesis in a hypothesis test; the power for a hypothesis test is equal to 1 - ß.
mean-difference size	The difference between the true population mean and the population mean associated with a false null hypothesis.
small mean-difference size	A situation where the sample mean does not deviate very much from the hypothesized population mean.

Formulas

z statistic for a hypothesis test on a population proportion $= z = \dfrac{P - p}{\sigma_P}$

z statistic for a hypothesis test on a population mean $= z = \dfrac{\overline{X} - \mu}{\sigma_{\overline{X}}}$

True/False Questions

____ 1. For a given significance level (such as $\alpha = .05$) it is easier to reject H_0 when you conduct a directional test of significance than when you conduct a nondirectional test.

____ 2. A researcher should wait until after the data are collected to decide whether a hypothesis test should directional or nondirectional.

____ 3. When a test statistic does not fall in the region for rejection the researcher can conclude that the null hypothesis is true.

____ 4. When a researcher reduces the alpha level in a hypothesis test from .05 to .01 he or she decreases the probability of making a Type II error.

____ 5. The probability of making a Type II error in a hypothesis test decreases as the size of the sample is increased.

____ 6. When a statistical decision to reject the null hypothesis is in error, the researcher has made a Type I error.

____ 7. When the null hypothesis is true, and a researcher fails to reject the null hypothesis on the basis of sample data, the probability of making a Type II error is equal to ß.

____ 8. Increasing the sample size is the only way to reduce the probability of **BOTH** a Type I and Type II error, at the same time.

____ 9. A statistically reliable result is a result that is likely to be repeated when a study is replicated by other researchers.

____ 10. In a hypothesis test, the value for z_{crit} is computed from the sample data.

____ 11. The region of rejection is the portion of the sampling distribution that represents significant outcomes.

____ 12. No matter how the null hypothesis (H_0) is stated, the alternative hypothesis (H_1) always states that the population parameter is not equal to a specified value (such as $\mu \neq 0$).

____ 13. When a researcher is only interested in whether sample data are significantly greater than hypothesized values, the entire region for rejection of the null hypothesis should be in the lower tail of the sampling distribution.

____ 14. When the results of a hypothesis test are reported the *p* value that is reported in the final conclusion is the same as the alpha level used in making the statistical decision.

Multiple Choice Questions

1. Which of the following will increase the power of a statistical test (decrease the probability of making a Type II error)?

   a. Increasing the size of the sample (*N*).
   b. Increasing the variability in the sample data.
   c. Increasing the level of significance (selecting a smaller value for α).
   d. All of the above will increase the power of a statistical test.

2. In a hypothesis test, the alternative hypothesis is

   a. not required when the null hypothesis is known to be false.
   b. only necessary when the hypothesis test is nondirectional.
   c. more sensitive than the null hypothesis to errors in the data set.
   d. the logical opposite to the null hypothesis.

3. A one-tailed or directional hypothesis test

   a. should only be used when the value of the sample statistic exceeds the value of the population mean.
   b. is preferred when there is a small mean-difference size.
   c. places the entire critical region into one tail of the sampling distribution.
   d. should be used whenever the sample size (*N*) is less than 30.

4. When a researcher rejects a null hypothesis that is actually false, the researcher

   a. should increase the sample size and conduct the hypothesis test again.
   b. has made a Type I error.
   c. has made a correct decision.
   d. has made a Type II error.

5. Martha is currently enrolled in a Political Science class. She had heard that in the past the average score for this class was 65% with a standard deviation of 9%. However, this year a new professor is teaching the class and the class average for the 36 students is 69%. Martha conducts a hypothesis test to determine if the new professor's grades are significantly different from previous classes. Based on the information provided, how should Martha present her final conclusion?

   a. There is no evidence the mean for this class differs significantly from 65, $z = 1.60$, $p > .05$.
   b. The mean for this class differs significantly from 65, $z = 1.60, p < .05$.
   c. The mean for this class differs significantly from 65, $z = 1.60, p > .05$.
   d. There is no evidence the mean for this class differs significantly from 65, $z = 1.60$, $p < .05$.

Matching Terms

____ 1.	beta	a.	failing to reject the null hypothesis when the null hypothesis is false
____ 2.	directional test	b.	theoretical value of a test statistic that would be required for significance
____ 3.	level of significance	c.	extreme portion of the sampling distribution that represents statistically significant outcomes
____ 4.	alternative hypothesis	d.	probability of correctly detecting and rejecting a false null hypothesis
____ 5.	Type II error	e.	hypothesis which states the observed outcome is due to chance variation
____ 6.	reliable	f.	probability level a researcher selects to assess the test statistic computed from a data set
____ 7.	region of rejection	g.	a research hypothesis in which the entire rejection region is located in one extreme of the sampling distribution
____ 8.	alpha level	h.	research outcome that is likely to be repeated if the study is replicated
____ 9.	statistically significant result	i.	probability of making a Type II error
____ 10.	critical value	j.	hypothesis which states the observed outcome is due to factors other than chance variation
____ 11.	null hypothesis	k.	rejecting the null hypothesis when the null hypothesis is true
____ 12.	Type I error	l.	a research hypothesis which has a rejection region in both extremes of the sampling distribution
____ 13.	power	m.	a test statistic that has an extremely low probability of occurrence in a distribution of chance events
____ 14.	nondirectional test	n.	probability of making a Type I error

Practice Problems

1. Using the following, calculate the value of the z test statistic:

When $\overline{X}$ is	σ is	N is, and	μ_0 is	z will be
39	7	100	35	
75	15	121	60	
108	20	25	80	
15	10	64	20	
1014	35	49	1050	
3	1	9	5	

2. Using the following, calculate the value of the z test statistic:

When P is	p is, and	N is	z will be
.79	.90	9	
.16	.05	64	
.63	.70	121	
.49	.45	25	
.98	.75	100	
.33	.50	49	

Chapter Review

Terminology

t statistic	A test statistic designed to be used instead of the *z* statistic whenever the population variance is unknown and must be estimated.
unbiased variance estimator	Sample statistic (s^2) whose long run, average value is exactly equal to the value of the population parameter σ^2; the value is derived by dividing the sum of squares for the sample by N - 1.
estimated standard error of the mean	The estimated standard deviation of the sampling distribution of $\overline{X}$.
degrees of freedom	The number of independent observations in the sample minus the number of parameters estimated in the formula; the standard abbreviation for degrees of freedom is *df*.

Formulas

Unbiased estimator of $\sigma^2 = s^2 = \dfrac{\Sigma(X-\overline{X})^2}{N-1}$ [Definitional formula]

Unbiased estimator of $\sigma^2 = s^2 = \dfrac{SS}{N-1}$ [**NOTE**: The formula for *SS* is in Chapter 4]

$$s_{\overline{X}} = \sqrt{\frac{s^2}{N}} = \frac{s}{\sqrt{N}}$$

t statistic for a hypothesis test on a population mean $= t = \dfrac{\overline{X}-\mu}{s_{\overline{X}}}$

t statistic for a hypothesis test on a correlation coefficient $= t = \dfrac{r\sqrt{N-2}}{\sqrt{1-r^2}}$

Confidence interval for the population mean $= \overline{X} \pm t_{\text{crit}}\, s_{\overline{X}}$

True/False Questions

____ 1. S^2 is a biased estimator of σ^2 because, in the long run, it underestimates the value of σ^2.

____ 2. The long run, expected value of the *t* distribution is equal to 1.0.

____ 3. A different *t* distribution exists for every particular sample size.

____ 4. When the size of a sample reaches 121, the *t* distribution is exactly equal to the standard normal distribution.

____ 5. The variance of the *t* distribution is equal to $(df - 2)/df$.

____ 6. Because the *t* distribution has a larger variance than the standard normal distribution, t_{crit} is always larger than the corresponding value for z_{crit} .

____ 7. When a *t* test requires a value for *df* that is not listed in a table of critical values, the value for the first available larger *df* is used.

____ 8. To determine the appropriate degrees of freedom for a sample statistic, the number of estimated parameters is subtracted from the total number of independent observations in a sample.

____ 9. As the degrees of freedom is increased the *t* distribution becomes flatter and has more variability.

____ 10. When the degrees of freedom is equal to 6 the *t* distribution is 1.5 times more variable than the standard normal distribution.

____ 11. The value of t_{crit} for a directional hypothesis test will always be less than the value for a nondirectional hypothesis test with the same degrees of freedom.

____ 12. In a directional hypothesis test, the absolute value of the *t* statistic is compared to the value of t_{crit}.

____ 13. Increasing the sample size will normally produce a smaller estimated standard error of the mean and a larger calculated value for the *t* statistic.

____ 14. When a researcher fails to reject the null hypothesis using $\alpha = .05$, the final write-up should include the statement $p > .05$.

____ 15. When the *t* statistic is used to test the significance of a correlation coefficient the degrees of freedom is equal to the number of paired observations minus 2 $(N - 2)$.

____ 16. The *t* statistic can be used to construct confidence intervals when the population variance is unknown.

Multiple Choice Questions

1. Sarah is conducting a learning experiment which involves timing rats running through a maze. For the 10 rats in her sample $\overline{X}$ = 51.3 seconds and s = 3 seconds. For Sarah's study, what would be the value of $s_{\overline{X}}$?

   a. 1.00
   b. 0.30
   c. 0.95
   d. 0.55

2. A group of researchers were investigating gender differences in interpersonal distance during face-to-face communication. In communications between members of the same sex the average distance is 24 inches. In a pilot study of 16 male-female couples, the average distance during face-to-face communication was 26 inches, with $s^2 = 4$. In testing for differences from the "norm" of 24 inches, what would be the value of the t-statistic for this data set?

   a. 2.00
   b. 3.87
   c. 1.97
   d. 4.00

3. Research on short-term memory capacity indicates that the average amount of information retained in short-term memory is 7.0 items. Dr. Wesley has recently developed a memory improvement program that should significantly enhance short-term memory. When the memory program was pilot tested 24 participants remembered an average of 8.1 items, with s = 3.4 items. Using $\alpha = .01$, calculate the t-statistic for this sample and decide if the average in Dr. Wesley's study is significantly higher than 7.0 items.

   a. t = 0.32, fail to reject the null hypothesis.
   b. t = 1.58, fail to reject the null hypothesis.
   c. t = 1.58, reject the null hypothesis.
   d. t = 2.92, reject the null hypothesis.

4. A group of researchers were investigating REM sleep in premature infants. As part of their research they timed the length of the first REM cycle of a sleep session for 12 infants and found the average was 16.00 minutes, with s = 1.5 minutes. Assuming the length of REM sleep cycles is normally distributed, construct a 95% confidence interval for the true population mean on the basis of this sample.

   a. 12.73 to 19.27
   b. 15.22 to 16.78
   c. 15.05 to 16.95
   d. 15.06 to 16.94

Matching Terms

____	1. SS	a.	number of independent observations in the sample minus the number of parameters estimated in the formula
____	2. H_1	b.	coefficient of determination
____	3. P	c.	sample variance
____	4. σ^2	d.	hypothesis indicating that a research outcome is produced by factors other than chance
____	5. r	e.	probability of making a Type II error
____	6. α	f.	sample proportion
____	7. z	g.	calculated value of test statistic when σ is unknown
____	8. S^2	h.	population proportion
____	9. $\sigma_{\overline{X}}$	i.	probability of making a Type I error
____	10. df	j.	sum of squares
____	11. z_{crit}	k.	hypothesis indicating that a research outcome does not differ from chance
____	12. t	l.	standard error of the mean
____	13. p	m.	theoretical value of test statistic when σ is known (derived from a table)
____	14. r^2	n.	estimated standard error of the mean
____	15. H_0	o.	unbiased estimator of population variance
____	16. t_{crit}	p.	correlation coefficient
____	17. ß	q.	theoretical value of test statistic when σ is unknown (derived from a table)
____	18. s^2	r.	population variance
____	19. $s_{\overline{X}}$	s.	calculated value of test statistic when σ is known

Practice Problems

1. Using the following, calculate the sum of squares (*SS*) and the unbiased estimator of σ^2 (s^2):

When ΣX is	and ΣX^2 is	and N is	SS will be	and s^2 will be
378	20622	13		
57	333	12		
449	24505	11		
386	26736	9		
129	3433	10		
502	32884	8		
96	1572	14		

2. Using the following, calculated the estimated standard error of the mean ($s_{\overline{X}}$):

When ΣX is	and ΣX^2 is	and N is	$s_{\overline{X}}$ will be
626	39496	15	
293	9409	11	
1677	221779	18	
47	351	9	
491	24479	12	
245	4343	20	
196	4578	10	

3. Using the following, calculate the value for the *t* statistic to test the hypothesized value of μ:

When ΣX is	ΣX^2 is	N is	and μ_0 is	t will be
679	38857	15	50	
246	6874	11	20	
2486	391004	18	135	
47	321	9	10	
425	20443	12	50	
261	4421	20	10	

4. Using the following, determine the value for t_{crit} the researcher should use:

When H_0 is	α is	and *N* is	t_{crit} will be
$\mu = 50$	.05	36	
$\mu \leq 150$	.01	12	
$\mu \geq 7.5$	.05	49	
$\mu = 400$	.01	24	
$\mu \leq 32$	.05	121	
$\mu \geq 0.5$	.01	61	

5. Using the following, calculate 95% confidence intervals for the population mean:

When $\overline{X}$ is,	s is,	and *N* is,	the 95% confidence interval for μ will be:
987	72	121	
12	3	64	
126	9	36	
48	12	81	
82	18	169	
9	1	4	

Chapter Review

Terminology

completely randomized two-group design	A research method in which each research participant is randomly assigned to one of two treatment conditions.
independent-samples *t* test	A statistical test designed to compare the sample means from the experimental and control conditions in a completely randomized two-group design.
sampling distribution of the mean difference	The sampling distribution for the test statistic in an independent-samples *t* test.
standard error of the mean difference	The standard deviation of the sampling distribution of $\overline{X}_1 - \overline{X}_2$.
pooled estimator of the population variance	The weighted average of the independent variance estimates from each sample in a completely randomized two-group experimental design.
homogeneity of variance assumption	The assumption that the variances in two populations are equal; it is reasonable to assume assumption is not violated if the larger of the two variance estimates is less than twice the size of the smaller estimate.
static-group comparison design	A two-group research design where a group of subjects who share a particular trait is compared on some dependent measure to a second group of subjects who do not possess the trait in question.
correlated-samples *t* test	A statistical test designed to compare the sample means from the experimental and control conditions when the data in the two conditions are correlated.
repeated-measures design	A research design in which each participant participates in both the experimental and the control conditions.
pretest score	The score a research participant receives on a dependent measure before he or she is exposed to the independent variable in an experiment.
posttest score	The score a research participant receives on a dependent measure after he or she is exposed to the independent variable in an experiment.

difference scores — The result obtained when the posttest score for a research participant is subtracted from his or her pretest score on the same measure.

sample mean of the difference scores ($\overline{D}$) — The mean value of the difference scores in a correlated-samples research design.

randomized matched-groups design — A research design in which pairs of subjects are formed by matching two participants at a time on some variable that is strongly correlated with the dependent measure in the study; once the matched pairs are formed one member from each pair is randomly assigned to the experimental condition and the other to the control condition.

error term — An index of random error in a research study.

Formulas

Estimated standard error of the mean difference = $s_{\overline{X}_1-\overline{X}_2} = \sqrt{s_p^2\left(\frac{1}{N_1}+\frac{1}{N_2}\right)}$

Pooled estimate of the population variance = $s_p^2 = \frac{(N_1-1)s_1^2+(N_2-1)s_2^2}{(N_1-1)+(N_2-1)}$

t statistic for a hypothesis test with two independent samples = $t = \frac{\overline{X}_1-\overline{X}_2}{s_{\overline{X}_1-\overline{X}_2}}$

Sample mean of the difference scores = $\overline{D} = \overline{X}_1 - \overline{X}_2$

Sum of squares of the difference scores = $SS = \Sigma D^2 - \frac{(\Sigma D)^2}{N}$

Unbiased estimate of $\sigma_D^2 = s^2 = \frac{SS}{N-1}$

Estimated standard error of $\overline{D} = s_{\overline{D}} = \sqrt{\frac{s^2}{N}}$

t statistic for a hypothesis test with two correlated samples = $t = \frac{\overline{D}}{s_{\overline{D}}}$

True/False Questions

____ 1. In an independent-samples research design the data in the control condition are completely independent of the data in the experimental condition.

____ 2. In a completely randomized two-group design, the two groups of participants are assumed to be statistically equivalent at the start of the study.

____ 3. The typical absolute mean difference in a one-sample statistical test is expected to be greater than the typical mean difference in a two-sample test.

____ 4. The standard error of the mean will be less than the standard error of the mean difference, when both are based on the same population variance and sample size.

____ 5. A significant difference between the two groups in a static-group comparison design provides evidence of a cause-and-effect relationship between the defining trait and the dependent measure.

____ 6. In general, a correlated-samples *t* test is more powerful (has a lower probability of a Type II error) than an equivalent independent-samples *t* test.

____ 7. A two-sample *t* test is appropriate for analyzing data measured on ordinal, interval or ratio scales.

____ 8. The homogeneity of variance assumption may be violated if the larger of the two variance estimates is more than twice the size of the smaller variance estimate.

____ 9. In general, the value of t_{crit} in a correlated-samples *t* test will be larger than the value of t_{crit} in an equivalent independent-samples *t* test.

____ 10. The unbiased variance estimator is an index of the variation with a sample due to random sampling error and experimental error.

____ 11. If a researcher completes a completely randomized two-group experimental study and discovers that the raw scores from the experimental group are strongly correlated with the raw scores from the control group, he or she should substitute the correlated-samples *t* test for the independent-samples *t* test in the data analysis.

____ 12. The correlated-samples t-test assumes that the D scores are normally distributed in the population represented by the sample.

____ 13. In a completely randomized two-group experimental design, both groups must have the same number of participants if the independent-samples *t* test is used to analyze the data.

Multiple Choice Questions

1. A researcher wants to determine the side-effects of a newly developed drug. Specifically, the researcher is investigating the drug's effect on memory. In the study 19 individuals are tested, and the number of errors each person makes in recalling a list of words is recorded. Nine subjects receive the drug under investigation and the remaining ten subjects are given a placebo. The researcher finds that for the experimental group the mean number of errors is $\overline{X}_1 = 10.0$, $s = 4.2$ errors; for the control group the mean number of errors is $\overline{X}_2 = 15.0$ errors, $s = 4.4$ errors. Calculate the value of $s_{\overline{X}_1 - \overline{X}_2}$ for this study.

   a. 3.92
   b. 0.95
   c. 4.33
   d. 1.98

2. Given the following summary statistics from a recent study:
   Experimental group: $\overline{X}_1 = 3.6$, s = 1.1, $N_1 = 16$
   Control group: $\overline{X}_2 = 4.8$, s = 2.3, $N_2 = 25$
   Calculate the value of the t-statistic for this study, and report whether the null hypothesis: $\mu_1 = \mu_2$ should be rejected, using $\alpha = .05$.

   a. $t = 2.791$; reject the null hypothesis.
   b. $t = 1.943$; rcjcct thc null hypothcsis.
   c. $t = 3.158$; fail to reject the null hypothesis.
   d. $t = 0.612$; fail to reject the null hypothesis.

3. Dr. Tang records the average number of errors an individual makes in reading aloud. Each participant is tested twice, once while he or she is alone and once while he or she is being observed by three other people. Dr. Tang subtracts the two scores for each participant and calculates the following sample statistics for the difference scores:
   $\overline{D} = 9.4$, $s^2 = 22.0$, $N = 25$.
   Calculate the value of the t-statistic to test the hypothesis that $\mu_D = 0$ for Dr. Tang's study.

   a. 2.136
   b. 0.401
   c. 10.020
   d. 0.427

Matching Terms

____	1. $s_{\overline{D}}$	a.	score a research participant receives prior to exposure to the independent variable
____	2. static-group comparison design	b.	statistical test that compares the sample means from the experimental and control conditions when the data in the two conditions are correlated
____	3. posttest score	c.	estimated standard error of $\overline{D}$
____	4. homogeneity of variance assumption	d.	weighted average of the independent variance estimates from the control and experimental groups
____	5. s_p^2	e.	research design where members of matched pairs are randomly assigned to either the experimental or the control condition
____	6. independent-samples *t* test	f.	research method in which research participants are randomly assigned to one of two treatment conditions
____	7. completely randomized two-group design	g.	research design where a group of subjects who share a particular trait is compared to a second group of subjects who do not possess the trait
____	8. correlated-samples *t* test	h.	assumption that the variances in two populations are equal
____	9. randomized matched-groups design	i.	score a research participant receives following exposure to the independent variable
____	10. $s_{\overline{X}_1 - \overline{X}_2}$	j.	pooled estimate of the population variance
____	11. pretest score	k.	statistical test that compares the sample means in a completely randomized two-group design

Practice Problems

1. Using the following, calculate the pooled estimate of the population variance (s_p^2) and the estimated standard error of the mean difference ($s_{\bar{X}_1-\bar{X}_2}$):

When s_1^2 is	N_1 is	s_2^2 is	and N_2 is	s_p^2 will be	and $s_{\bar{X}_1-\bar{X}_2}$ will be
10.26	10	7.42	10		
25.31	24	30.08	22		
101.42	36	85.13	30		
0.57	12	0.76	12		
48.69	19	45.11	24		
2.01	8	3.50	7		

2. Using the following, calculate the value for a independent-samples t statistic:

When $\bar{X}_1$ is	N_1 is	$\bar{X}_2$ is	N_2 is	and s_p^2 is	t will be
10.21	12	11.58	12	8.06	
28.56	24	19.83	25	2.64	
0.98	36	0.24	34	0.64	
40.67	10	43.94	10	3.87	
101.25	14	95.72	12	13.24	
1.03	20	1.59	24	4.51	

3. Using the following, calculate the value for a correlated-samples t statistic:

When $\bar{X}_1$	$\bar{X}_2$	N is	and s^2 is	t will be
11.54	13.97	12	20.96	
25.62	22.28	25	63.18	
1.07	2.14	36	0.81	
51.48	49.36	10	6.49	
147.39	150.02	40	22.53	
7.26	5.59	20	2.37	

4. Using the following, determine the value for t_{crit} the researcher should use:

When H_0 is	α is	N_1 is	and N_2 is	t_{crit} will be
$\mu_1 = \mu_2$	.05	36	36	
$\mu_D = 0$	.05	12	12	
$\mu_1 = \mu_2$	.05	24	22	
$\mu_D = 0$	.01	10	10	
$\mu_1 = \mu_2$	.01	20	24	
$\mu_D = 0$	.01	64	64	

Chapter Review

Terminology

completely randomized independent-samples design	A research design in which participants are randomly assigned to one of the treatment conditions, and each participant is tested in only one of the conditions.
analysis of variance (ANOVA)	A statistical procedure that simultaneously tests the significance of all possible mean differences within a given set of sample means.
omnibus test	A statistical test that is capable of detecting any and all possible differences within a given set of means.
testwise error rate	The probability of making a Type I error on any one statistical test (such as a *t* test); in general, the testwise error rate is equal to the stated alpha level.
family wise error rate	The probability of making a Type I error in repeated tests on the same set of sample statistics; for paired comparisons the family wise error rate is $1 - (1 - \alpha)^C$, where C is equal to the total number of comparisons.
one-factor ANOVA	A statistical method that can be used to analyze the data from a multiple condition experimental study which has only one independent variable.
F ratio	A statistic whose numerator is a measure of the variance that results from differences between treatment groups and whose denominator is a measure of the variance that results from differences within treatment groups.
grand mean ($\overline{X}_G$)	Weighted average of all the separate treatment means.
mean square	The value that results when a sum of squares (*SS*) is divided by the appropriate degrees of freedom (*df*).
N	The number of independent observations in <u>each</u> treatment group of a multiple condition experiment.
N_{tot}	The total number of independent observations in the experiment; the value will be equal to ΣN.
k	The number of treatment groups within a multiple condition experiment.

analysis of variance summary table	A device for displaying the results of an ANOVA.
total sum of squares	A measure of the variation of all the raw scores in a data set around the grand mean of the entire data set.
within-treatments sum of squares	A measure of the random variation among the participants within each of the treatment conditions.
between-treatments sum of squares	A measure of the variation among the sample means from the various treatment conditions.
pairwise comparisons	A method for assessing the significance of differences between the means in a multiple condition experiment by comparing two means at a time.
Tukey's honestly significant difference (*HSD*)	The minimum significant mean difference in a set of means; allows all possible pairwise comparisons while holding the probability of a Type I error at the stated alpha level.
a priori test	Testing one sample mean against another to assess a specific hypothesis that existed prior to the collection of the data.
post hoc comparison	Testing one sample mean against another, following the preliminary data analysis, when no specific paired differences were anticipated prior to the collection of the data.
eta-squared (η^2)	The proportion of variance in the dependent variable that is explained by the independent variable *for the sample of data used.*

Formulas

Sums of squares for a one-factor ANOVA [Computational formulas]:

$$SS_{\text{tot}} = \Sigma X^2 - \frac{(\Sigma X)^2}{N_{\text{tot}}}$$ [Using <u>all</u> the raw scores in the <u>entire</u> data set]

$$SS_B = \Sigma[N(\overline{X} - \overline{X}_{\text{G}})^2]; \text{ where } \overline{X}_{\text{G}} = \frac{\Sigma X}{N_{\text{tot}}}$$

$$SS_W = SS_{\text{tot}} - SS_B$$

Degrees of freedom for a one-factor ANOVA:

$$df_{\text{tot}} = N_{\text{tot}} - 1$$

$$df_B = k - 1$$

$$df_W = N_{\text{tot}} - k$$

Mean squares for a one-factor ANOVA:

$$MS_B = \frac{SS_B}{df_B}$$

$$MS_W = \frac{SS_W}{df_W}$$

F statistic for a one-factor ANOVA = $F = \dfrac{MS_B}{MS_W}$

Minimum significant difference between two means (post hoc):

Tukey test: $HSD = q\sqrt{\dfrac{MS_W}{N}}$

Scheffé test: $S = \sqrt{(df_B)(F_{\text{crit}})(MS_W)\left(\dfrac{1}{N_i} + \dfrac{1}{N_j}\right)}$

Proportion of variance accounted for in the sample = $\eta^2 = \dfrac{SS_B}{SS_{\text{tot}}}$

True/False Questions

____ 1. An analysis of variance (ANOVA) test will only produce a significant result if all the means in a given set of means differ significantly from each other.

____ 2. The mean square within treatments is assumed to represent only random error variation.

____ 3. The computed value of an F statistic in a one-factor ANOVA should never be less than 1.0.

____ 4. When all the treatment groups in a one-factor, multiple condition experiment are the same size, MS_W will be equal to the average of the variance estimates from each of the treatment groups.

____ 5. Generally speaking, a Tukey *HSD* test should be used to follow-up any one-factor ANOVA, regardless of the outcome of the initial F test.

____ 6. The *HSD* post hoc test is less conservative and has more power than the Scheffé post hoc test.

____ 7. Eta-squared only provides an estimate of the explained variance in the sample, not in the overall population from which the sample was drawn.

____ 8. A one-factor ANOVA procedure assumes that the independent variable is measured on either an interval or ratio scale.

____ 9. An ANOVA ensures that the family wise error rate will be equal to the stated level of α, regardless of the number of treatment groups being compared.

____ 10. In determining the critical value for F two degrees of freedom are required; the degrees of freedom for the numerator is $k - 1$ and the degrees of freedom for the denominator is $N_{tot} - k$.

____ 11. In a one-factor ANOVA the total degrees of freedom (df_{tot}) is always equal to the sum of the between-treatments and within-treatments degrees of freedom ($df_B + df_W$).

____ 12. A significant result in the "omnibus F test" indicates that all the sample means being compared differ significantly from each other.

____ 13. A pairwise comparison is a test that assesses the significance of the difference between two means at a time.

____ 14. A researcher who uses a standard two-sample t statistic to conduct post hoc testing increases the likelihood of making a Type I error beyond the stated alpha level for the study.

Multiple Choice Questions

1. In a one-factor ANOVA the total sum of squares (SS_{tot}) is represented by the formula

   a. $\Sigma(X - \overline{X}_G)^2$
   b. $N\Sigma(X - \overline{X}_G)^2$
   c. $N\Sigma(\overline{X} - \overline{X}_G)^2$
   d. $\Sigma(X - \overline{X}_G)$

2. In a one-factor ANOVA the between-treatments sum of squares (SS_B) represents

   a. variations in the data set due to individual differences between the participants.
   b. the total variation present in the overall data set.
   c. variability due to the experimental treatments.
   d. variability between participants within each of the different experimental conditions.

3. Dr. Carmichael sets up an experiment with 60 participants. There are 5 different treatment conditions, with 12 participants in each condition. In Dr. Carmichael's experiment, how many degrees of freedom will there be for SS_B?

   a. 55
   b. 48
   c. 11
   d. 4

4. For a typical one-factor ANOVA which of the following statements will be true concerning the mean square estimates of variance?

   a. the value of MS_B will be smaller than the value of MS_W.
   b. the value of MS_W will be smaller than the value of MS_B.
   c. the values of MS_B and MS_W will be identical.
   d. It is impossible to make general statements about these two values; either one may be the larger of the two values.

5. Dr. Santos sets up an experiment involving a total of 66 participants. There are 6 different treatment conditions, with 11 participants in each condition. If Dr. Santos uses $\alpha = .05$ to test a null hypothesis: $\mu_1 = \mu_2 = \mu_3 = \mu_4 = \mu_5 = \mu_6$, what is the critical value from the F table that should be used to evaluate the final F statistic?

   a. 3.12
   b. 2.37
   c. 2.25
   d. 3.34

Matching Terms

____	1. analysis of variance	a.	probability of making a Type I error on any one statistical test
____	2. pairwise comparisons	b.	statistical test capable of detecting all possible differences within a given set of means
____	3. total sum of squares	c.	minimum significant mean difference in a set of means
____	4. completely randomized independent-samples design	d.	comparing two sample means to assess a specific hypothesis that existed prior to collection of the data
____	5. post hoc comparison	e.	measure of the variation of all the raw scores in a data set around the grand mean of the entire data set
____	6. testwise error rate	f.	probability of making a Type I error in repeated tests on the same set of sample statistics
____	7. within-treatments sum of squares	g.	simultaneously testing the significance of all possible mean differences within a given set of sample means
____	8. Tukey's honestly significant difference	h.	measure of the random variation among the participants within each of the treatment conditions
____	9. between-treatments sum of squares	i.	comparing two sample means when no specific differences were anticipated prior to collection of the data
____	10. a priori test	j.	method for assessing the significance of differences between the means by comparing two means at a time
____	11. omnibus test	k.	measure of the variation among the sample means from the various treatment conditions
____	12. family wise error rate	l.	research design in which each participant is randomly assigned to only one of the treatment conditions

Practice Problems

1. Using the following, determine df_B, df_W, and the value for F_{crit} when $\alpha = .05$:

When N_{tot} is	and k is	df_B will be	df_W will be	and F_{crit} will be
36	4			
54	3			
60	6			
100	5			
72	3			
64	4			
90	6			

2. Using the following, calculate the value for Tukey's *HSD* when $\alpha = .05$:

When MS_W is	N is	k is	and df_W is	*HSD* will be
128.19	60	4	56	
1.04	30	5	25	
0.90	42	3	39	
2235.33	21	3	18	
9.48	27	3	24	
72.75	40	4	36	

3. Using the following, calculate the value for Scheffé's critical difference when $\alpha = .05$ (assume all the treatment groups are the same size):

When df_B is	df_W is	MS_W is	and N is	S will be
3	56	7.67	60	
2	39	1.91	42	
4	25	1034.76	30	
3	24	98.47	28	
2	36	156.25	39	
3	76	49.13	80	

Chapter Review

Terminology

factorial design	A research design that has two independent variables and all designated levels of one independent variable are combined with all designed levels of the second independent variable.
main effect	The effect of one of the independent variables in a two-way factorial design when the influence of the second independent variable is held constant statistically.
interaction effect	The joint effect of the two independent variables in a two-way factorial research design.
factorial experiment	A factorial research design in which participants are randomly assigned to the various levels of at least one of the independent variables in the study.
completely randomized factorial experiment	A factorial research design in which subjects are randomly assigned to the various levels of both independent variables, and each participant serves in only one of the possible treatment combinations.
mixed factorial design	A factorial research design in which subjects are randomly assigned to the various levels of one independent variable but not the other.

Formulas

Sums of squares for a two-way ANOVA [Computational formulas]:

$$SS_{\text{tot}} = \Sigma X^2 - \frac{(\Sigma X)^2}{N_{\text{tot}}}$$ [Using all the raw scores in the entire data set]

$$SS_{\text{between treatments}} = \Sigma[N(\overline{X}_{AB} - \overline{X}_{\text{G}})^2];\ \text{where } \overline{X}_{\text{G}} = \frac{\Sigma X}{N_{\text{tot}}}$$

$$SS_A = \Sigma[bN(\overline{X}_A - \overline{X}_{\text{G}})^2]$$
$$SS_B = \Sigma[aN(\overline{X}_B - \overline{X}_{\text{G}})^2]$$
$$SS_{AxB} = SS_{\text{between treatments}} - SS_A - SS_B$$

$$SS_{\text{within treatments}} = SS_{\text{tot}} - SS_{\text{between treatments}}$$

Degrees of freedom for a two-way ANOVA:

$$df_{\text{tot}} = N_{\text{tot}} - 1$$

$$df_A = a - 1$$

$$df_B = b - 1$$

$$df_{AxB} = (a - 1)(b - 1)$$

$$df_W = ab(N - 1)$$

Mean squares for a two-way ANOVA:

$$MS_A = \frac{SS_A}{df_A}$$

$$MS_B = \frac{SS_B}{df_B}$$

$$MS_{AxB} = \frac{SS_{AxB}}{df_{AxB}}$$

$$MS_{\text{within treatments}} = \frac{SS_{\text{within treatments}}}{df_{\text{within treatments}}}$$

F statistics for a two-way ANOVA:

Main effect of factor *A*: $F_A = \dfrac{MS_A}{MS_{\text{within treatments}}}$

Main effect of factor *B*: $F_B = \dfrac{MS_B}{MS_{\text{within treatments}}}$

*A*x*B* interaction effect: $F_{AxB} = \dfrac{MS_{AxB}}{MS_{\text{within treatments}}}$

Proportion of variance accounted for by each factor and the interaction = $\eta^2 = \dfrac{SS_{\text{effect}}}{SS_{\text{tot}}}$

True/False Questions

____ 1. In a two-way ANOVA with 3 levels of factor *A* and 4 levels of factor *B*, there will be a total of 6 treatment groups.

____ 2. In a two-way ANOVA a main effect refers to the effect of one independent variable when the other independent variable is held constant statistically.

____ 3. When the mean difference associated with one of the factors in a two-way ANOVA changes in direction across levels of the second factor the two variables interact with each other.

____ 4. In a two-way ANOVA it is possible for factor *A* to interact with factor *B* without having factor *B* interact with factor *A*.

____ 5. In a two-way ANOVA it is possible to have a significant *A*x*B* interaction when neither factor *A* nor factor *B* has a significant main effect.

____ 6. As a general rule, when the plot of a variable's means produces a function that is not parallel to the *X* axis, there is no main effect for that variable.

____ 7. As a general rule, any time a plot of the means from various treatment combinations results in steeply crossed functions, it is likely that there is an interaction between the two factors in the study.

____ 8. In a two-way ANOVA three separate hypotheses are evaluated and for each hypothesis there may be a different value for F_{crit}.

____ 9. In a two-way ANOVA there is a secondary partitioning of the variance in which the within-treatments sum of squares is broken down into sums of squares for factor *A* , factor *B*, and an *A*x*B* interaction.

____ 10. In a two-way ANOVA the number of treatment groups (and the number of treatment means that can be compared) is equal to *a•b*.

____ 11. In a two-way ANOVA post hoc testing using Tukey's *HSD* can be carried out if either of the main effects is significant or if the interaction effect is significant.

____ 12. When there is a large overall mean difference between two conditions in a factorial experiment it indicates the main effect will be significant when an analysis of variance is carried out.

____ 13. If both main effects are significant, but there is no interaction between the factors, the lines on a graph plotting the means for each of the treatment conditions will be parallel to each other.

Multiple Choice Questions

1. The main advantage for researchers who use a factorial design in an experiment is

   a. the between condition variability is reduced making the statistical test more powerful.
   b. in addition to testing the main effects for each independent variable it is possible to test for interactions between the independent variables.
   c. factorial designs permit the researcher to carry out longitudinal testing, one-way designs only allow cross-sectional testing.
   d. the within condition variability is reduced making the statistical test more powerful.

2. When two variables interact it means that

   a. an increase in one of the variables will cause in an increase in the second variable.
   b. a decrease in one of the variables will cause in an increase in the second variable.
   c. the effect of one variable is influenced by changes in the second variable.
   d. the effect of each variable is independent and changing the level of one variable has no effect on the second variable.

3. Researchers were studying the effect of being observed on the speed of decisions in preschoolers (Group 1) and adolescents (Group 2). If the following graph were representative of the results of the study, which statement would provide the most accurate description of the study's outcome?

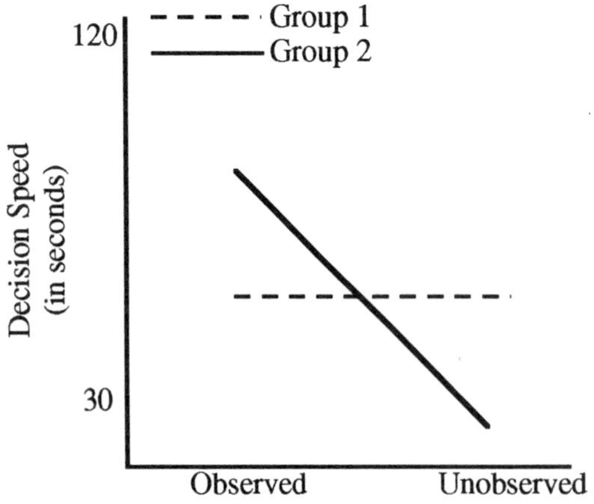

   a. There is a main effect for age, but there is no effect for observed/unobserved and no interaction.
   b. There is a main effect for observed/unobserved and an interaction between age and observed/unobserved, but there is no effect for age.
   c. There are main effects for age and observed/unobserved, but there is no interaction.
   d. There is an interaction, but there is no main effect for age or observed/unobserved.

Matching Terms

____	1. completely randomized factorial experiment	a.	effect of one of the independent variables in a factorial design when the influence of the second independent variable is held constant statistically
____	2. MS_B	b.	research design in which subjects are randomly assigned to the various levels of one independent variable but not the other
____	3. main effect	c.	The variance in a data set that is attributable to Factor *A*, on its own
____	4. $MS_{\text{within treatments}}$	d.	joint effect of the two independent variables in a factorial research design
____	5. mixed factorial design	e.	research design with two independent variables where all designated levels of one independent variable are combined with all designated levels of the second independent variable
____	6. MS_A	f.	The variance in a data set that is assumed to come from sampling error and experimental error
____	7. factorial design	g.	The variance in a data set that is attributable to Factor *B*, on its own
____	8. interaction effect	h.	research design in which subjects are randomly assigned to the various levels of both independent variables

Practice Problems

1. Using the following, determine df_A, df_B, df_{AxB}, and df_W (assume all treatment groups are the same size):

When *N* is	*a* is	and *b* is	df_A will be	df_B will be	df_{AxB} will be	and df_W will be
120	3	4				
72	2	3				
80	4	5				
150	5	2				

Chapter Review

Terminology

within-subjects experimental design	A research design where each subject is tested at all levels of the independent variable; in a repeated-measures ANOVA there is only one independent variable, but each subject provides data in all the different experimental conditions.

Formulas

Sums of squares for a repeated-measures ANOVA [Computational formulas]:

$$SS_{\text{tot}} = \Sigma X^2 - \frac{(\Sigma X)^2}{N_{\text{tot}}}$$ [Using all the raw scores in the entire data set]

$$SS_{\text{between treatments}} = \Sigma[N(\overline{X} - \overline{X}_G)^2]; \text{ where } \overline{X}_G = \frac{\Sigma X}{N_{\text{tot}}}$$

$$SS_{\text{within treatments}} = SS_{\text{tot}} - SS_{\text{between treatments}}$$

$$SS_{\text{between subjects}} = \Sigma[k(\overline{X}_{\text{subject}} - \overline{X}_G)^2]$$

$$SS_{\text{subjects x treatments}} = SS_{\text{within treatments}} - SS_{\text{between subjects}}$$

Degrees of freedom for a repeated-measures ANOVA:

$$df_{\text{tot}} = N_{\text{tot}} - 1$$

$$df_{\text{between treatments}} = k - 1$$

$$df_{\text{between subjects}} = N - 1$$

$$df_{\text{subjects x treatments}} = (k - 1)(N - 1)$$

Mean squares for a repeated-measures ANOVA:

$$MS_{\text{effect}} = MS_{\text{between treatments}} = \frac{SS_{\text{between treatments}}}{df_{\text{between treatments}}}$$

$$MS_{\text{error}} = MS_{\text{subjects x treatments}} \ \frac{SS_{\text{subjects x treatments}}}{df_{\text{subjects x treatments}}}$$

F statistic for a repeated-measures ANOVA = $\dfrac{MS_{\text{effect}}}{MS_{\text{error}}} = \dfrac{MS_{\text{between treatments}}}{MS_{\text{subjects x treatments}}}$

Proportion of explained variance accounted = $\eta^2 = \dfrac{SS_{\text{effect}}}{SS_{\text{tot}}}$

Minimum significant difference between two means (Tukey test): $HSD = q\sqrt{\dfrac{MS_{\text{error}}}{N}}$

True/False Questions

____ 1. In a repeated-measures ANOVA the null hypothesis states that all the treatment means will be equal.

____ 2. In a repeated-measures ANOVA one critical assumption is that the raw-score difference between any two subjects will remain approximately constant at all levels of the independent variable.

____ 3. Experimental error includes random differences that result from procedural factors and random differences that occur due to naturally occurring individual differences between research participants.

____ 4. In a repeated-measures ANOVA, if the error term were not partitioned into two separate components the *F* statistic a researcher calculates would tend to be larger than it should be.

____ 5. To the extent that the assumption of no subjects x treatment interaction is met, a repeated-measures ANOVA will be more powerful than a standard one-way ANOVA.

____ 6. Carryover effects occur when a subject's responses in one experimental condition are influenced by the other conditions he or she has been exposed to in the same experiment.

____ 7. All research questions that involve multiple conditions can be accurately tested using either an independent-samples design or a repeated-measures design.

____ 8. Whenever a statistically significant result is obtained in ANOVA the researcher can conclude that the independent variable produces more than half the observed variation in the dependent variable.

Multiple Choice Questions

1. Professor Kahn sets up a repeated-measures experiment with 20 participants who take part in each of 5 different treatment conditions. For this experiment how many degrees of freedom are in the denominator of $MS_{\text{subjects x treatment}}$?

   a. 23
   b. 19
   c. 4
   d. 76

2. In a repeated-measures ANOVA the $\text{MS}_{\text{subjects x treatment}}$ for a data set provides an unbiased estimator of

   a. the variation within the data set that is due to individual differences.
   b. the variation within the data set that is due to treatment effects.
   c. error variation within the data set once the variability due to individual differences among subjects is removed.
   d. the total variation within the data set.

3. In comparing a repeated measures design with an independent-groups design (involving the same data set) which of the following statements would be true?

   a. The value of SS_{tot} will be smaller in a repeated-measures design than in an independent groups design.
   b. The value of the error term in the denominator of the *F* statistic will be smaller in a repeated-measures design than in an independent-groups design.
   c. The value of the numerator of the *F* statistic will be smaller in a repeated-measures design than in an independent groups design.
   d. The value of the error term in the denominator of the *F* statistic will be smaller in a independent-groups design than in an repeated-measures design.

4. Dr. Macobi designs a repeated-measures experiment with 4 different experimental conditions. If there are 10 participants in the experiment and $\alpha = .05$, which of the following statements provides the correct values for the *F* test?

   a. The degrees of freedom are 3, 36; the critical value for the *F* statistic is 2.92.
   b. The degrees of freedom are 3, 6; the critical value for the *F* statistic is 4.76.
   c. The degrees of freedom are 3, 9; the critical value for the *F* statistic is 3.86.
   d. The degrees of freedom are 3, 27; the critical value for the *F* statistic is 2.96.

Matching Terms

____ 1.	SS_A	a.	measure of the variation in the various treatment means around the grand mean of the entire data set
____ 2.	$SS_{\text{between subjects}}$	b.	measure of the variation in a data set with two independent variables, that is attributable to Factor *B*
____ 3.	SS_{tot}	c.	proportion of variance in the dependent variable that is explained by the independent variable (within a data set)
____ 4.	SS_{AxB}	d.	measure of the variation of all the raw scores in a data set around the grand mean of the entire data set
____ 5.	$SS_{\text{within treatments}}$	e.	measure of the variation in a data set, with two independent variables, that is attributable to the combined effects of Factors *A* and *B*
____ 6.	SS_B	f.	measure of only the random variation in the raw scores due to procedural factors such as equipment malfunctions or misunderstood instructions
____ 7.	$SS_{\text{subjects x treatments}}$	g.	measure of the variation in a data set, with two independent variables, that is attributable to Factor *A*
____ 8.	η^2	h.	measure of the random variation due to individual differences among the participants in each condition
____ 9.	$SS_{\text{between treatments}}$	i.	measure of the variation in the raw scores around the separate treatment means for each of the conditions

Practice Problems

1. Using the following, determine the value for $SS_{\text{subjects x treatments}}$:

When SS_{tot} is	$SS_{\text{between treatments}}$ is	and $SS_{\text{between subjects}}$ is	$SS_{\text{subjects x treatments}}$ is
4962	951	3600	
512	112	295	
98	34	51	
3457	492	2847	
946	82	618	
2971	496	1489	

2. Using the following, calculate the value for the F statistic:

When $SS_{\text{between treatments}}$ is	$SS_{\text{subjects x treatments}}$ is	k is	and N is	F will be
901	411	4	10	
98	186	5	16	
52	35	3	40	
347	1104	3	24	
1025	496	3	35	
126	264	4	8	

3. Using the following, calculate the value for Tukey's HSD when $\alpha = .05$:

When $SS_{\text{subjects x treatments}}$ is	N is	and k is	HSD will be
126	12	4	
15	8	5	
63	20	3	
2196	30	3	
94	14	3	
229	24	4	

Chapter Review

Terminology

parametric tests	Statistical procedures used to assess the equivalence of specific population parameters.
nonparametric tests	Statistical procedures used to assess the equivalence of whole distributions.
robustness	The degree to which a statistical test yields accurate results even when one of its assumptions is violated.
frequency count	The number of observations within a data set that fall into a particular nominal-scale category.
chi-square test	A nonparametric statistical procedure used to compare observed frequency counts to expected frequency counts.
goodness-of-fit test	A nonparametric statistical procedure used to assess whether the observed pattern of frequency counts fit a distribution of frequency counts specified in advance.
observed frequency	The actual number of observations that occur in a particular nominal category.
expected frequency	The number of observations predicted to occur in a particular nominal category based on a model distribution.
test of association	A nonparametric statistical procedure used to assess whether there is a reliable association between two variables; also known as a *test of independence*.
contingency table	A display listing the frequency counts for each level and each possible combination of two variables.
cells	The individual boxes in a frequency table that contain the actual frequency counts.
row total	The sum of the frequency counts of all the cells that are in a particular row of a frequency table.
column total	The sum of the frequency counts of all the cells that are in a particular column of a frequency table.

grand total	The sum of the frequency counts in all the cells of a frequency table.
phi coefficient	A nonparametric equivalent of the Pearson *r* that can be calculated when the data set involves frequency count data in a 2 x 2 contingency table.
Mann-Whitney *U* test	A nonparametric statistical procedure used to assess the significance of differences between two independent samples; used primarily when data are measured on an ordinal scale.
normal approximation of the *U* distribution	A special procedure used to convert a *U* score to a *z* score when the number of observations in both samples is equal to or greater than 20.
Wilcoxen *T* test	A nonparametric statistical procedure used to assess the significance of differences between two correlated samples; used primarily when data are measured on an ordinal scale.

Formulas

Goodness-of-fit test

$$\text{Chi-square} = \chi^2 = \sum\left[\frac{(f_o - f_e)^2}{f_e}\right]$$

Expected frequency = f_e = (theoretical proportion)(N), where $N = \sum f_o$

degrees of freedom = $df = (c - 1)$, where c = number of nominal categories

Test of association

$$\text{Chi-square} = \chi^2 = \sum\left[\frac{(f_o - f_e)^2}{f_e}\right]$$

$$\text{Expected frequency} = f_e = \frac{\text{row total x column total}}{N}$$

degrees of freedom = $df = (r - 1)(c - 1)$, where r = number of rows and c = number of columns

Phi coefficient = $\varphi = \sqrt{\dfrac{\chi^2}{N}}$; φ^2 is an index of effect size in a 2 x 2 contingency table

Mann-Whitney U test

$$\text{Shared rank of tied scores} = \frac{\text{sum of rank positions held by tied scores}}{\text{number of tied scores}}$$

Sum of ranks for group A = ΣR_A = total of all ranks for individuals in Group A

Sum of ranks for group B = ΣR_B = total of all ranks for individuals in Group B

$$U_A = N_A N_B + \frac{N_A(N_A+1)}{2} - \Sigma R_A$$

$$U_B = N_A N_B + \frac{N_B(N_B+1)}{2} - \Sigma R_B$$

U = Min (U_A, U_B)

NOTE: The null hypothesis is rejected if the calculated value for $U \le U_{crit}$

Normal approximation of the U distribution

$$\mu = \frac{N_A N_B}{2}$$

$$\sigma = \sqrt{\frac{N_A N_B(N_A + N_B + 1)}{12}}$$

$$z_U = \frac{U - \mu}{\sigma}$$

Wilcoxen T test

$$\text{Shared rank of tied scores} = \frac{\text{sum of rank positions held by tied scores}}{\text{number of tied scores}}$$

Sum of positive ranks = ΣR_+ = total of all ranks where difference is >0

Sum of negative ranks = ΣR_- = total of all ranks where difference is <0

T = Min (R_+, R_-)

NOTE: The null hypothesis is rejected if the calculated value for $T \le T_{crit}$

True/False Questions

____ 1. In a nonparametric test the null hypothesis will be rejected if the distributions being compared are significantly different in center, variability, skewness or shape.

____ 2. Nonparametric tests can be used when the assumption that the observations in the data sample are independent of one another is violated.

____ 3. For nonparametric tests to be valid the data being analyzed should be measured on either an interval or ratio scale.

____ 4. In general, nonparametric procedures are less powerful than their parametric counterparts, and as a consequence there is a higher probability of making a Type II error.

____ 5. For every possible degrees of freedom there is a different sampling distribution for chi-square.

____ 6. In a goodness-of-fit test, the null hypothesis will be rejected if the computed value for χ^2 is less than or equal to χ^2_{crit}.

____ 7. A correlation exists within a contingency table when at least one level of one of the variables is associated with a particular level of the second variable more often than would be expected on the basis of chance.

____ 8. One limitation on the chi-square test is that the observed frequencies for all cells should be equal to or greater than 5.

____ 9. The Mann-Whitney *U* test is primarily sensitive to a difference between the medians in two independent samples.

____ 10. In the Wilcoxen *T* test the null hypothesis will be rejected if the computed value for the test statistic is less than or equal to the value of T_{crit}.

____ 11. Difference scores of 0 are not included in the sum of ranks for a Mann-Whitney *U* test.

____ 12. The value for T_{crit} in the Wilcoxen procedure is determined by the total number of pairs in the data set, including any pairs where the difference is scores is equal to 0.

____ 13. Nonparametric tests are principally substituted for parametric tests when the assumptions of interval data and/or normal population cannot be satisfied.

____ 14. When the null hypothesis is rejected in a χ^2 test of association it indicates the two variables being assessed are significantly correlated with each other.

Multiple Choice Questions

1. Professor Washburn surveyed a child development class at the end of the school term to determine which section of the course student enjoyed the most. In a class of 36 students 12 students preferred the section on infancy and preschoolers, 8 preferred the section on ages 6-12, and 16 preferred the section on adolescence. Assuming students have no real preference for any one section of the course, what is the value of the χ^2 statistic for this data set?

   a. 0.313
   b. 3.000
   c. 0.222
   d. 2.667

2. Dr. Montgomery surveys 400 men and women asking whether they support or oppose a particular political candidate. When the data are summarized in a 2 x 2 contingency table the value for χ^2 is 8.40. Calculate the effect size for Dr. Montgomery's data set.

   a. The value of φ is 0.14, indicating 14% of the variation in one variable can be accounted for by the second variable.
   b. The value of φ is 0.42, indicating 42% of the variation in one variable can be accounted for by the second variable.
   c. The value of φ^2 is 0.18, indicating 18% of the variation in one variable can be accounted for by the second variable.
   d. The value of φ^2 is 0.02, indicating 2% of the variation in one variable can be accounted for by the second variable.

3. A researcher has pretest and posttest data from 6 subjects, and the data are measured on an ordinal scale. The most appropriate statistical testing procedure would be

   a. the χ^2 test of association.
   b. the Wilcoxen *T* test.
   c. the Mann-Whitney *U* test.
   d. the normal approximation of the *U* distribution.

4. Dr. Jansen had a group of 200 business managers and 200 college professors complete the Myers-Briggs personality inventory, which categorizes individuals into 1 of 16 different personality types. In Dr. Jansen's study how many degrees of freedom would there be in a χ^2 test of association?

   a. 15
   b. 1
   c. 398
   d. It is impossible to determine without additional information.

Matching Terms

____ 1. chi-square test	a.	degree to which a statistical test yields accurate results even when one of its assumptions is violated
____ 2. nonparametric tests	b.	nonparametric statistical procedure used to assess whether the observed pattern of frequency counts fit a specified distribution of frequency counts
____ 3. expected frequency	c.	nonparametric statistical procedure used to assess whether there is a reliable association between two variables
____ 4. robustness	d.	nonparametric equivalent of the Pearson *r* calculated for frequency count data in a 2 x 2 contingency table
____ 5. test of association	e.	statistical procedures used to assess the equivalence of population parameters
____ 6. Wilcoxen *T* test	f.	nonparametric statistical procedure used to compare observed and expected frequency counts
____ 7. goodness-of-fit test	g.	nonparametric statistical procedure used to assess differences between two independent samples
____ 8. Mann-Whitney *U* test	h.	statistical procedures used to assess the equivalence of complete distributions
____ 9. phi coefficient	i.	actual number of observations that occur in a particular nominal category
____ 10. parametric tests	j.	nonparametric statistical procedure used to assess differences between two correlated samples
____ 11. observed frequency	k.	number of observations predicted to occur in a particular nominal category

Practice Problems

1. Using the following, determine the expected frequency of the each event:

When the population proportion is	and N individuals are tested	the expected frequency count will be
0.15	400	
0.72	60	
0.33	40	
0.49	32	
0.02	81	
0.65	144	

2. Using the following, determine the value of U:

When N_A is	N_B is	ΣR_A is	and ΣR_B is	U will be
8	4	36	42	
9	6	81	39	
10	8	69	102	
6	9	62	58	
4	10	40	65	
7	7	71	34	
15	12	126	252	

This chapter provides a summary of the formulas that are used in inferential statistics.

Prediction and Estimation

In linear regression, the values of the dependent or criterion variable (Y) are predicted based on the relationship between Y and the independent or predictor variable (X).

The formula used to predict values of Y is:

$$Y' = bX + a$$

$$b = r\,(S_Y / S_X)$$

$$a = \overline{Y} - b\overline{X}$$

$$r = \frac{CP_{XY}}{\sqrt{SS_X \bullet SS_Y}}$$

$$S_Y = \sqrt{S_Y^2}$$

$$S_X = \sqrt{S_X^2}$$

$$\overline{Y} = \frac{\Sigma Y}{N}$$

$$\overline{X} = \frac{\Sigma X}{N}$$

$$CP_{XY} = \Sigma(XY) - \frac{(\Sigma X \bullet \Sigma Y)}{N}$$

$$SS_X = \Sigma X^2 - \frac{\Sigma(X)^2}{N}$$

$$SS_Y = \Sigma Y^2 - \frac{(\Sigma Y)^2}{N}$$

$$S_Y^2 = \frac{SS_Y}{N}$$

$$S_X^2 = \frac{SS_X}{N}$$

With <u>interval estimation</u> a range of values is calculated that has a specified, long-run probability of containing the true value of the population parameter being estimated. The most common intervals are those estimating means and those estimating proportions.

The formula for the confidence interval used to estimate the population mean when the population variance (σ^2) is known is:

$$\overline{X} \pm z_c \sigma_{\overline{X}}$$

$$\overline{X} = \frac{\Sigma X}{N}$$

$$\sigma_{\overline{X}} = \sqrt{\frac{\sigma^2}{N}} = \frac{\sigma}{\sqrt{N}}$$

The formula for the confidence interval used to estimate the population mean when the population variance (σ^2) is unknown is:

$$\overline{X} \pm t_{\text{crit}} s_{\overline{X}}$$

$$\overline{X} = \frac{\Sigma X}{N}$$

$$s_{\overline{X}} = \sqrt{\frac{s^2}{N}} = \frac{s}{\sqrt{N}}$$

$$s^2 = \frac{SS}{N-1}$$

$$SS = \Sigma X^2 - \frac{\Sigma(X)^2}{N}$$

The formula for the confidence interval used to estimate a population proportion is:

$$P \pm z_c \sigma_P$$

$$\sigma_P = \sqrt{\frac{pq}{N}}; \text{ where } q = (1 - p)$$

Testing Significance

Tests of significance are conducted to statistically evaluate hypotheses concerning the characteristics of a population. The assessment is based on the values of test statistics that are derived from data collected from a representative sample of the overall population.

One-Sample Tests

The formula for the statistic used to compare the mean from a sample to a specified value for μ when the population variance (σ^2) is known is:

$$z = \frac{\overline{X} - \mu}{\sigma_{\overline{X}}}$$

$$\overline{X} = \frac{\Sigma X}{N}$$

$$\sigma_{\overline{X}} = \sqrt{\frac{\sigma^2}{N}} = \frac{\sigma}{\sqrt{N}}$$

The formula for the statistic used to compare the mean from a sample to a specified value for μ when the population variance (σ^2) is unknown is:

$$t = \frac{\overline{X} - \mu}{s_{\overline{X}}}$$

$$\overline{X} = \frac{\Sigma X}{N}$$

$$s_{\overline{X}} = \sqrt{\frac{s^2}{N}} = \frac{s}{\sqrt{N}}$$

$$s^2 = \frac{SS}{N-1}$$

$$SS = \Sigma X^2 - \frac{\Sigma(X)^2}{N}$$

The formula for the statistic used to compare the proportion in a sample to a specified population proportion is:

$$z = \frac{P - p}{\sigma_P}$$

$$\sigma_P = \sqrt{\frac{pq}{N}}\text{; where } q = (1 - p)$$

The formula for the statistic used to assess whether the correlation coefficient calculated for a sample differs significantly from zero (no correlation) is:

$$t = \frac{r\sqrt{N-2}}{\sqrt{1-r^2}}$$

$$r = \frac{CP_{XY}}{\sqrt{SS_X \bullet SS_Y}}$$

$$CP_{XY} = \Sigma(XY) - \frac{(\Sigma X \bullet \Sigma Y)}{N}$$

$$SS_X = \Sigma X^2 - \frac{\Sigma(X)^2}{N}$$

$$SS_Y = \Sigma Y^2 - \frac{(\Sigma Y)^2}{N}$$

The formula for the statistic used to assess whether the pattern of frequency counts observed in a sample fits a theoretical distribution of frequency counts is:

$$\text{Chi-square} = \chi^2 = \sum\left[\frac{(f_o - f_e)^2}{f_e}\right]$$

$$f_e = (\text{theoretical proportion})(N)$$

Two-Sample Tests

The formula for the statistic used to compare the means from two independent samples measured on an interval or ratio scale, and drawn from a population that is not highly skewed is:

$$t = \frac{\overline{X}_1 - \overline{X}_2}{s_{\overline{X}_1 - \overline{X}_2}}$$

$$s_{\overline{X}_1 - \overline{X}_2} = \sqrt{s_p^2\left(\frac{1}{N_1} + \frac{1}{N_2}\right)}$$

$$s_p^2 = \frac{(N_1 - 1)s_1^2 + (N_2 - 1)s_2^2}{(N_1 - 1) + (N_2 - 1)}$$

$$s_1^2 = \frac{SS_1}{N_1 - 1}$$

$$s_2^2 = \frac{SS_2}{N_2 - 1}$$

$$SS_1 = \Sigma X_1^2 - \frac{\Sigma(X_1)^2}{N_1}$$

$$SS_2 = \Sigma X_2^2 - \frac{\Sigma(X_2)^2}{N_2}$$

The calculations for the statistic used to compare the means from two independent samples measured on an ordinal scale, or drawn from a population that is highly skewed are:

$$U = \text{Min}\,(U_A, U_B)$$

$$U_A = N_A N_B + \frac{N_A(N_A + 1)}{2} - \Sigma R_A$$

$$U_B = N_A N_B + \frac{N_B(N_B + 1)}{2} - \Sigma R_B$$

ΣR_A = total of all ranks for individuals in Group A

ΣR_B = total of all ranks for individuals in Group B

The formula for the statistic used to <u>compare the means from two correlated samples measured on an interval or ratio scale</u>, and drawn from a population that is not highly skewed is:

$$t = \frac{\overline{D}}{s_{\overline{D}}}$$

$$\overline{D} = \overline{X}_1 - \overline{X}_2$$

$$s_{\overline{D}} = \sqrt{\frac{s^2}{N}}$$

$$\overline{X}_1 = \frac{\Sigma X_1}{N_1}$$

$$\overline{X}_2 = \frac{\Sigma X_2}{N_2}$$

$$s^2 = \frac{SS_D}{N-1}$$

$$SS_D = \Sigma D^2 - \frac{(\Sigma D)^2}{N}$$

The calculations for the statistic used to <u>compare the means from two correlated samples measured on an ordinal scale</u>, or drawn from a population that is highly skewed are:

$T = \text{Min}\ (R_+, R_-)$

ΣR_+ = total of all ranks where difference is >0

ΣR_- = total of all ranks where difference is <0

The formula for the statistic used to <u>assess whether there is a reliable association between two variables</u> which are both measured on a nominal scale is:

$$\text{Chi-square} = \chi^2 = \sum\left[\frac{(f_o - f_e)^2}{f_e}\right]$$

$$f_e = \frac{\text{row total x column total}}{N}$$

Tests Involving More Than Two Samples

When more than two samples are being compared and the data are measured on an interval or ratio scale, the typical statistical method used to compare the means from the different samples is an analysis of variance (ANOVA). All ANOVA procedures start with three basic calculations:

$$SS_{\text{tot}} = \Sigma X^2 - \frac{(\Sigma X)^2}{N_{\text{tot}}}$$ [Using all the raw scores in the entire data set]

$$SS_{\text{between treatments}} = \Sigma[N(\bar{X}_i - \bar{X}_G)^2$$

$$\bar{X}_i = \frac{\Sigma X_i}{N_i}$$

$$\bar{X}_G = \frac{\Sigma X}{N_{\text{tot}}}$$

ΣX_i = sum of the raw scores in each treatment condition

$$SS_{\text{within treatments}} = SS_{\text{tot}} - SS_{\text{between treatments}}$$

When there is a single independent variable, different participants in each of the treatment conditions, and the participants are randomly assigned, a one-way ANOVA is the appropriate procedure to use. The calculations involved in a one-way ANOVA are:

$$F = \frac{MS_{\text{between treatments}}}{MS_{\text{within treatments}}}$$

$$MS_{\text{between treatments}} = \frac{SS_{\text{between treatments}}}{df_{\text{between treatments}}}$$

$$MS_{\text{within treatments}} = \frac{SS_{\text{within treatments}}}{df_{\text{within treatments}}}$$

$$df_{\text{between treatments}} = k - 1$$

$$df_{\text{within treatments}} = N_{\text{tot}} - k$$

When there is a <u>single independent variable but the same participants are tested in each of the treatment conditions</u> a repeated-measures ANOVA is the appropriate procedure to use. In a repeated-measures ANOVA $SS_{\text{within treatments}}$ is partitioned into two separate components prior to the calculation of the *F* statistic. The calculations involved in a repeated-measures ANOVA are:

$$SS_{\text{within treatments}} = SS_{\text{tot}} - SS_{\text{between treatments}}$$

$$SS_{\text{between subjects}} = \Sigma[k(\overline{X}_{\text{subject}} - \overline{X}_{\text{G}})^2]$$

$$\overline{X}_{\text{subject}} = \frac{\Sigma X_{\text{subject}}}{N_k}$$

$$\overline{X}_{\text{G}} = \frac{\Sigma X}{N_{\text{tot}}}$$

$\Sigma X_{\text{subject}}$ = sum of the raw scores for each subject

N_k = number of treatment conditions

$$SS_{\text{subjects x treatments}} = SS_{\text{within treatments}} - SS_{\text{between subjects}}$$

$$F = \frac{MS_{\text{between treatments}}}{MS_{\text{subjects x treatments}}}$$

$$MS_{\text{between treatments}} = \frac{SS_{\text{between treatments}}}{df_{\text{between treatments}}}$$

$$MS_{\text{subjects x treatments}} = \frac{SS_{\text{subjects x treatments}}}{df_{\text{subjects x treatments}}}$$

$$df_{\text{between treatments}} = k - 1$$

$$df_{\text{subjects x treatments}} = (k - 1)(N - 1)$$

When there are two independent variables, different participants in each of the treatment conditions, and the participants are randomly assigned, a two-way ANOVA is the appropriate procedure to use. In a two-way ANOVA $SS_{\text{between treatments}}$ is partitioned into three separate components, and three separate F statistics are calculated. The calculations involved in a two-way ANOVA are:

$$SS_{\text{between treatments}} = \Sigma[N(\overline{X}_i - \overline{X}_G)^2$$

$$\overline{X}_i = \frac{\Sigma X_i}{N_i}$$

$$\overline{X}_G = \frac{\Sigma X}{N_{\text{tot}}}$$

ΣX_i = sum of the raw scores in each treatment condition

$$SS_A = \Sigma[bN(\overline{X}_A - \overline{X}_G)^2]$$

$$SS_B = \Sigma[aN(\overline{X}_B - \overline{X}_G)^2]$$

$$SS_{AxB} = SS_{\text{between treatments}} - SS_A - SS_B$$

$$\overline{X}_A = \frac{\Sigma X_{ai}}{N_{ai}}$$

$$\overline{X}_B = \frac{\Sigma X_{bi}}{N_{bi}}$$

$$\overline{X}_G = \frac{\Sigma X}{N_{\text{tot}}}$$

ΣX_{ai} = sum of raw scores in each level of Factor A

N_{ai} = total observations at each level of Factor A

ΣX_{bi} = sum of raw scores in each level of Factor B

N_{bi} = total observations at each level of Factor B

$$F_A = \frac{MS_A}{MS_{\text{within treatments}}}$$

$$F_B = \frac{MS_B}{MS_{\text{within treatments}}}$$

$$F_{AxB} = \frac{MS_{AxB}}{MS_{\text{within treatments}}}$$

$$MS_A = \frac{SS_A}{df_A}$$

$$MS_B = \frac{SS_B}{df_B}$$

$$MS_{AxB} = \frac{SS_{AxB}}{df_{AxB}}$$

$$MS_{\text{within treatments}} = \frac{SS_{\text{within treatments}}}{df_{\text{within treatments}}}$$

$$df_A = a - 1$$

$$df_B = b - 1$$

$$df_{AxB} = (a - 1)(b - 1)$$

$$df_W = ab(N - 1)$$

When an ANOVA indicates there are significant differences among the means post hoc pairwise comparisons are usually made and the explained variation is usually calculated. Two statistics that can be used for these purposes are:

$HSD = q\sqrt{\frac{MS_{\text{error}}}{N}}$; MS_{error} is from the denominator of the *F* statistic

$\eta^2 = \frac{SS_{\text{effect}}}{SS_{\text{tot}}}$; SS_{effect} is used to calculate the numerator of the F statistic

Chapter 2 - Basic Concepts and Ideas

True/False Questions

1 - F It is not necessary to study the entire population, but the *sample that is selected should be representative and unbiased*
2 - T
3 - T
4 - F The actual raw score that is received is the *value* of the variable
5 - F If one variable contributes to or causes a change in another variable, those variables have a *causal* relationship
6 - F A correlational research design will only allow a researcher to determine if two variables covary; it *does not allow an inference about cause-and-effect*
7 - T
8 - T
9 - F The dependent variable is the variable that is *measured* by the researcher; the variable that is systematically manipulated is the independent variable
10 - F Subjects are *not randomly assigned in a correlational study*; the variables are measured as they occur, without manipulation or random assignment
11 - T
12 - T
13 - F Prior to conducting any mathematical analyses, the raw scores are referred to as the *data set*
14 - T
15 - T

Multiple Choice Questions

1 - C
2 - A This study is correlational research because the relationship between two variables is being investigated, but there is no active manipulation of either variable
3 - B The temperature of the room differs between the two groups, so it is the independent variable; the dependent variable would be the level of aggression at the end of the study
4 - B The number of bar presses can be accurately counted so this would be a quantitative variable
5 - D Descriptive statistics describe a given data set; inferential statistics use the data from a sample to extrapolate to a larger population

Matching Terms

1 - c; 2 - f; 3 - e; 4 - n; 5 - b; 6 - j; 7 - l; 8 - m; 9 - h; 10 - i; 11 - d; 12 - k; 13 - g; 14 - a

Chapter 3 - Frequency Distributions and Graphs

True/False Questions

1 - T
2 - F With ordinal measurement the scores can only be *rank ordered*; mathematical differences between scores are not meaningful
3 - F A scale must have *an absolute zero point* to be a ratio scale
4 - T
5 - T
6 - F A grouped frequency distribution can be created for *any type of data*
7 - T
8 - T
9 - T
10 - F Cumulative relative frequencies represent the percent of scores below the *exact upper limit* of a class interval
11 - T
12 - F With nominal data the category labels should be arranged *alphabetically*
13 - T
14 - T
15 - F Bar graphs are used with nominal data; *histograms are used with ordinal, interval or ratio data*
16 - T

Multiple Choice Questions

1 - B Ordinal scales allow only rank ordering of scores within a data set
2 - B The exact lower limit of a class interval is 1/2 unit of measurement below the stated lower limit; data are measured to 1/10 so limit will be 0.5/10 below the stated limit
3 - C The number of class intervals should be between 6 and 20
4 - A Exact Range = (96 - 59) + 1 = 38
5 - A

Matching Terms

1 - k; 2 - n; 3 - d; 4 - e; 5 - i; 6 - f; 7 - l; 8 - h; 9 - m; 10 - b; 11 - g; 12 - c; 13 - o; 14 - j; 15 - a

Practice Problems

(1)

Class Interval	Midpoint of Interval	Exact Lower Limit	Exact Upper Limit
70 to 90	80	69.5	90.5
10.2 to 10.8	10.5	10.15	10.85
2 to 7	4.5	1.5	7.5
1.50 to 1.54	1.52	1.495	1.545
-10 to -4	-7	-10.5	-3.5
-1.0 to +1.0	0	-1.05	+1.05

(2)

Raw Score	Frequency	Relative Frequency
92	7	0.0875
91	9	0.1125
90	0	0.0000
89	1	0.0125
88	10	0.1250
87	20	0.2500
86	12	0.1500
85	2	0.0250
84	8	0.1000
83	11	0.1375

(3)

Lowest Value in Data Set	Highest Value in Data Set	Range	Exact Range
35	97	62	63
2.1	5.3	3.2	3.3
101	624	523	524
-6	0	6	7
5.95	11.57	5.62	5.63
72	149	77	78
8.4	11.0	2.6	2.7

(4)

Raw Score	Frequency	Relative Cumulative Frequency
115-119	25	0.2083
110-114	19	0.3667
105-109	14	0.4833
100-104	10	0.5667
95-99	0	0.5667
90-94	8	0.6333
85-89	5	0.6750
80-84	1	0.6833
75-79	18	0.8333
70-74	20	1.0000

Chapter 4 - Summary Measures

True/False Questions

1 - F The mode is the *most frequently occurring value*; the median is the midpoint of the distribution (*50th percentile*)
2 - F The use of the median as a measure of central tendency depends on the *level of measurement and the shape of the distribution*, not the number of observations
3 - T
4 - T
5 - F A measure of *central tendency cannot be meaningfully calculated for nominal data*; typically the mode (most common value) is reported
6 - T
7 - T
8 - F Even when the mean and median values for two samples are identical, the *samples can still differ in their dispersion or spread*
9 - T
10 - F As variation increases the *semi-interquartile range also tends to increase*
11 - T
12 - F Deviation scores should always *sum to zero*
13 - T
14 - T
15 - F *Variance is reported in squared units*, not the same unit as the raw data; the measure of variation that is in the same units as the raw data is the *standard deviation*
16 - F There is *no meaningful measure of dispersion for nominal data*; the number of categories is usually reported to indicate the range of possible values

Multiple Choice Questions

1 - B The median score is the midpoint of the data set; it is <u>not</u> derived mathematically and therefore its value is relatively unaffected by extreme scores in the distribution
2 - B The two middle scores are 3 and 7; the median will be the average of these two values: $(3 + 7) / 2 = 5$
3 - A The interquartile range contains the central 50% of the scores in a distribution; the semi-interquartile range is equal to one-half the interquartile range
4 - B
5 - A In a unimodal distribution, when the mean for the distribution is greater than the median, there is generally a concentration of scores toward the low end of the distribution and fewer scores toward the high end of the distribution; this pattern of skew is a positive skew

Matching Terms

1 - e; 2 - l; 3 - g; 4 - i; 5 - d; 6 - m; 7 - k; 8 - n; 9 - f; 10 - c; 11 - j; 12 - h; 13 - p; 14 - o; 15 - b; 16 - a

Practice Problems

(1) The mode is the most frequently occurring value in the data set

a. 33
b. 104
c. 5
d. no mode exists
e. 44

(2) The median is the middle score in a data set with an odd number of observations, and the average of the two middle scores in a data set with an even number of observations

a. 57
b. 29
c. 3.5
d. 37
e. 42

(3) The mean is the arithmetic average of a data set

a. 34.62
b. 42.89
c. 5.42
d. 14.33
e. 45.64

(4)

When ΣX is	and ΣX^2 is	and N is	SS will be	S^2 will be	and S will be
378	20622	13	9630.92	740.84	27.22
57	333	12	62.25	5.19	2.28
449	24505	11	6177.64	561.60	23.70
386	26736	9	10180.89	1131.21	33.63
129	3433	10	1768.90	176.89	13.30
502	32884	8	1383.50	172.94	13.15
96	1572	14	913.71	65.27	8.08

Chapter 5 - Relative Measures and the Normal Curve

True/False Questions

1 - T
2 - F The raw score (or percent) that an individual receives on an exam only indicates individual performance; *percentile rank indicates relative standing relative to others who took the same exam*; these two values are seldom the same
3 - T
4 - T
5 - F Changing the scale of measurement from raw scores to *z* scores *will not affect the shape of the distribution in any way*
6 - T
7 - F The standard normal distribution is open-ended and the endpoints of the distribution are $\pm\infty$ (infinity).
8 - T
9 - F Using *z* scores and the standard normal distribution to estimate percentile ranks is based on the assumption that the underlying distribution is distributed in the same way as the normal curve (symmetrical and bell-shaped).

Multiple Choice Questions

1 - C Transforming a set of raw scores to *z* scores does not change the shape of the original distribution of scores
2 - C Converting the *z* scores back to raw scores shows that Mary earned 2(5) + 60 = 70; Jack earned 1.5(2) + 67 = 70.
3 - B Sue Ann's score was 5 points above the mean (1/2 a standard deviation); therefore her *z* score would be +0.50
4 - C
5 - D

Matching Terms

1 - f; 2 - e; 3 - a; 4 - c; 5 - b; 6 - d

Practice Problems

(1)

When $\overline{X}$ is	and S is,	a raw score of	will convert to a z score of:
97	9.23	100	+0.33
46	8.01	38	-1.00
8	0.52	9	+1.92
22	1.37	24	+1.46
31	4.69	24	-1.49
54	7.15	39	-2.10
100	6.48	110	+1.54
75	3.74	73	-0.53

(2)

Between z =	and z =	the proportion of the normal distribution is:
+0.57	$+\infty$	0.2843
$-\infty$	- 1.36	0.0869
-1.21	-0.46	0.2097
$-\infty$	+0.12	0.5478
-0.61	$+\infty$	0.7291
+1.85	+1.99	0.0089
-0.29	+0.97	0.4481

(3)

A z score of	has a percentile rank of:
+0.69	75
-1.12	13
-3.37	0
+2.57	99
-2.02	2
+3.12	100
+1.58	94
-0.74	23

(4)

When $\overline{X}$ is	and S is,	a z score of	will correspond to a raw score of:
28	5.17	-1.62	20
69	2.35	+2.58	75
7	0.86	+1.05	8
41	4.73	-2.37	30
72	1.07	+0.41	72
85	3.21	-3.19	75
150	9.61	-0.26	148
36	6.59	+3.70	60

Chapter 6 - Linear Correlation

True/False Questions

1 - T
2 - F A high positive correlation indicates that *X* and *Y* tend to change in the same direction, but it *does not indicate which variable causes the change* to occur
3 - F As long as variables have a *relatively linear* relationship the Pearson *r* can be used
4 - T
5 - T
6 - F A low value of *r* only indicates a weak linear relationship; the variables *may have a strong curvilinear relationship*
7 - F The Pearson *r assumes the paired data have a relatively linear relationship*
8 - F The nature of the relationship (direct or inverse) is *independent of the strength of the relationship*
9 - T
10 - T
11 - F When *comparing correlations the value of* r^2 *should be used*; a correlation of -0.60 is approximately <u>four</u> times as strong as a correlation of +0.36
12 - T
13 - F A meaningful correlation coefficient *can be calculated for variables measured on any scale*
14 - T
15 - F The *sign* of a correlation coefficient only *indicates the direction* of the relationship; the *absolute value* of the correlation coefficient *indicates the strength* of the relationship
16 - T

Multiple Choice Questions

1 - C The absolute value of *r* can range from 0.00 to 1.00 and the higher the value, the stronger the relationship between the two variables
2 - A A scatterplot that goes down and to the right indicates an inverse relationship exists between the two variables
3 - B The positive sign indicates the two variables will change in the same direction, the amount of predictable change would be equal to $+0.66^2$, or approximately 44%
4 - C

Matching Terms

1 - l; 2 - h; 3 - g; 4 - j; 5 - i; 6 - k; 7 - d; 8 - b; 9 - c; 10 - a; 11 - e; 12 - f

Practice Problems

(1)

When ΣX is,	ΣX^2 is,	ΣY is,	ΣY^2 is,	ΣXY is,	and N is,	r will be
595	42803	638	44422	36006	11	+0.17
495	32803	464	26568	18399	12	-0.07
532	38834	289	9683	16449	15	+0.68
586	42722	595	42803	31220	10	-0.46
501	33967	495	32803	1562	20	-0.52
289	9683	501	33967	11017	17	+0.26

Chapter 7 - Linear Regression

True/False Questions

1 - T
2 - F When $r = 0.00$, the best prediction for every X value *is* $z'_Y = 0.00$
3 - T
4 - T
5 - F The intercept is the point where the regression line *crosses the Y axis*
6 - F Because the value of the slope is used as a multiplier, the value should be reported to *3, and preferably 4 decimal places*
7 - T
8 - T
9 - T
10 - F When the prediction equation is more accurate the *data points will be clustered closer to the regression line*; as the scatter increases, the accuracy of the prediction is decreased
11 - F The homoscedasticity assumption *will be violated if the amount of scatter* <u>*does*</u> *vary* from one value for *Y'* to the next
12 - F This statement reflects the *bivariate normality assumption*, the linearity assumption states that variables *X* and *Y* have a straight line relationship
13 - T
14 - T
15 - T
16 - F The explained variance provides an estimate of the variance that can be accounted for, but it *cannot be used to make a causal statement*
17 - F The coefficient of determination provides an estimate of the variation in variable *Y* that is *accounted for by variable X*

Multiple Choice Questions

1 - D The highest absolute value for *r* indicates the strongest correlation, and as the strength of the correlation increases the value of the prediction errors will decrease
2 - B When the value of *r* is increased the value of the prediction errors will decrease
3 - D
4 - C The final term is the value of the intercept which is the point where the regression line will cross the *Y* axis
5 - A

Matching Terms

1 - f; 2 - c; 3 - j; 4 - l; 5 - b; 6 - i; 7 - d; 8 - k; 9 - g; 10 - a; 11 - h; 12 - e

Practice Problems

(1)

When *b* is	and *X*	*Y* will
+0.56	increases 5 units	increase 2.80 units
-2.36	increases 4 units	decrease 9.44 units
+1.24	decreases 10 units	decrease 12.40 units
-7.01	decreases 2 units	increase 14.02 units
+3.71	increases 1 units	increase 3.71 units
-1.69	increases 7 units	decrease 11.83 units
+2.17	decreases 6 units	decrease 13.02 units
-0.52	decreases 11 units	increase 5.72 units
+5.63	increases 8 units	increase 45.04 units
-0.47	increases 12 units	decrease 5.64 units
+0.98	decreases 9 units	decrease 8.82 units
-4.82	decreases 3 units	increase 14.46 units

(2)

When S_X is	and S_Y is	and *r* is	the slope will be
2.34	17.91	+0.12	+0.9185
11.59	1.43	-0.46	-0.0568
5.67	4.86	+0.85	+0.7286
8.47	3.72	-0.27	-0.1186
7.13	12.54	+0.63	+1.1080
9.26	0.69	-0.90	-1.0671

(3)

When $\overline{Y}$ is	and $\overline{X}$ is	and b is	the intercept will be
11.61	17.22	-3.45	71.02
27.37	1.98	+0.14	27.09
100.87	50.03	-0.98	149.90
0.54	4.61	+2.83	-12.51
54.19	0.87	-1.16	55.20
72.25	49.58	+1.27	9.28

(4)

When S_Y is	and r^2 is	and N is	$S_{est.Y}$ will be
1.64	+0.96	25	0.34
7.35	+0.18	40	6.83
2.87	+0.43	36	2.23
3.02	+0.54	60	2.08
10.49	+0.21	12	10.21
5.10	+0.75	100	2.58

Chapter 8 - Sampling Distributions

True/False Questions

1 - T
2 - F To assume the sampling distribution of $\overline{X}$ is normal, N should be at least 30
3 - F *Smaller samples* are affected more by extreme scores and therefore *give less precise estimates* of μ
4 - T
5 - T
6 - F The confidence level indicates the *long-run probability* that a specific interval size will contain the true population parameter, *not the probability for a single interval*
7 - F When sampling "with replacement" *the same observation can be included more than once* in the data set
8 - F As N increases the distribution for sample means will become bell-shaped, *regardless of the shape of the distribution for the sample data*
9 - T
10 - T
11 - F As the value of z_c increases *confidence intervals become wider and less precise*
12 - T
13 - T
14 - T

Multiple Choice Questions

1 - B
2 - D
3 - A
4 - A This is solved using the formula for the standard error of the mean, substituting in the values of σ and $\sigma_{\overline{X}}$, and solving for N
5 - C The interval limits are found using $52 \pm 1.96(\sigma_{\overline{X}})$

Matching Terms

1 - k; 2 - l; 3 - g; 4 - i; 5 - f; 6 - b; 7 - j; 8 - d; 9 - h; 10 - c; 11 - e; 12 - a

Practice Problems

(1)

When $\overline{X}$ is,	σ is,	and N is,	the 95% confidence interval for μ will be:
1096	72	121	1083.17 to 1108.83
16	4	64	15.02 to 16.98
140	10	36	136.73 to 143.27
50	10	81	47.82 to 52.18
90	28	169	85.78 to 94.22
7	2	4	5.04 to 8.96

(2)

When $\overline{X}$ is,	σ is,	and N is,	the 99% confidence interval for μ will be:
2543	41	81	2531.25 to 2554.75
25	8	4	14.68 to 35.32
107	12	36	101.84 to 112.16
48	7	49	45.42 to 50.58
89	15	64	84.16 to 93.84
11	3	121	10.30 to 11.70

(3)

When P is,	and N is,	the 95% confidence interval for the population proportion will be:
0.25	36	0.09 to 0.41
0.49	81	0.38 to 0.60
0.87	64	0.75 to 0.99
0.50	4	0.01 to 0.99
0.09	121	0.00 to 0.18
0.61	49	0.47 to 0.75

Chapter 9 - Logic of Hypothesis Testing

True/False Questions

1 - T
2 - F The null hypothesis should always be stated *in advance*, before data are collected
3 - F A researcher can *never prove a null hypothesis is true*; a non-significant result indicates there is support for the assumption that the observed outcome is due to chance variation
4 - F As the alpha level is reduced the *probability of making a Type II increases*
5 - T
6 - T
7 - F When H_0 is true and the researcher fails to reject H_0, *he or she has made a correct decision*; an error is only made when the statistical decision is incorrect
8 - T
9 - T
10 - F The value for z_{crit} is *determined using a table of statistical values*
11 - T
12 - F H_1 only has a not equal sign ($\neq$) *when the hypothesis being tested is nondirectional*
13 - F The entire rejection region would be in the *upper tail of the sampling distribution*
14 - T

Multiple Choice Questions

1 - A Increasing *N* will increase the power of the test, the other two alternatives will decrease the power of the statistical test
2 - D
3 - C
4 - C When a false H_0 is rejected the researcher has not made an error; the only errors that can be made are failing to reject a false H_0 or rejecting a true H_0
5 - A Because the computed value of z is less than z_{crit} (1.96) H_0 is not rejected and the correct probability to report is $p > .05$ (the α level for the hypothesis test)

Matching Terms

1 - i; 2 - g; 3 - f; 4 - j; 5 - a; 6 - h; 7 - c; 8 - n; 9 - m; 10 - b; 11 - e; 12 - k; 13 - d; 14 - l

Practice Problems

(1)

When $\overline{X}$ is	σ is	N is, and	μ_0 is	z will be
39	7	100	35	+5.71
75	15	121	60	+11.00
108	20	25	80	+7.00
15	10	64	20	-4.00
1014	35	49	1050	-7.20
3	1	9	5	-6.00

(2)

When P is	p is, and	N is	z will be
.79	.90	9	-1.10
.16	.05	64	4.04
.63	.70	121	-1.68
.49	.45	25	0.40
.98	.75	100	5.31
.33	.50	49	-2.38

Chapter 10 - One-Sample *t* Statistic

True/False Questions

1 - T
2 - F The long run, *expected value of the t distribution is 0.0*
3 - T
4 - F The *t* distribution is not exactly equal to the standard normal *until N reaches infinity*
5 - F The variance is $df/(df - 2)$
6 - T
7 - F The value for the *first available smaller df* should be used
8 - T
9 - F The *t* distribution will be flatter and more variable *as df is reduced*
10 - T
11 - T
12 - F In a directional hypothesis test *the sign for the calculated test statistic is important* because the entire region of rejection is in one tail of the sampling distribution
13 - T
14 - T
15 - T
16 - T

Multiple Choice Questions

1 - C The value for *s* is divided by the square root of the sample size
2 - D
3 - B
4 - C

Matching Terms

1 - j; 2 - d; 3 - f; 4 - r; 5 - p; 6 - i; 7 - s; 8 - c; 9 - l; 10 - a; 11 - m; 12 - g; 13 - h; 14 - b; 15 - k; 16 - q; 17 - e; 18 - o; 19 - n

Practice Problems

(1)

When ΣX is	and ΣX^2 is	and N is	SS will be	and s^2 will be
378	20622	13	9630.92	802.58
57	333	12	62.25	5.66
449	24505	11	6177.64	617.76
386	26736	9	10180.89	1272.61
129	3433	10	1768.90	196.54
502	32884	8	1383.50	197.64
96	1572	14	913.71	70.29

(2)

When ΣX is	and ΣX^2 is	and N is	$s_{\overline{X}}$ will be
626	39496	15	7.98
293	9409	11	3.82
1677	221779	18	14.63
47	351	9	1.21
491	24479	12	5.77
245	4343	20	1.88
196	4578	10	2.86

(3)

When ΣX is	ΣX^2 is	N is	and μ_0 is	t will be
679	38857	15	50	-0.761
246	6874	11	20	+0.669
2486	391004	18	135	+0.249
47	321	9	10	-4.664
425	20443	12	50	-2.282
261	4421	20	10	+1.866

(4)

When H_0 is	α is	and N is	t_{crit} will be
$\mu = 50$	.05	36	$\|2.042\|$
$\mu \leq 150$	.01	12	+2.718
$\mu \geq 7.5$	.05	49	-1.684
$\mu = 400$	.01	24	$\|2.807\|$
$\mu \leq 32$	.05	121	+1.658
$\mu \geq 0.5$	.01	61	-2.390

(5)

When $\overline{X}$ is,	s is,	and N is,	the 95% confidence interval for μ will be:
987	72	121	974.04 to 999.96
12	3	64	11.25 to 12.75
126	9	36	122.94 to 129.06
48	12	81	45.33 to 50.67
82	18	169	79.26 to 84.74
9	1	4	7.41 to 10.59

Chapter 11 - Two-Sample *t* Tests

True/False Questions

1 - T
2 - T
3 - F The typical absolute mean difference will be greater in a two-sample test *because the means can vary randomly on either side of the population mean*, not just one side
4 - T
5 - F A static-group comparison design is a *correlational research design* and it does not allow cause-and-effect conclusions to be inferred
6 - T
7 - F The *t* test is *only appropriate for data measured on interval or ratio scales*
8 - T
9 - T
10 - T
11 - F The *procedure and experimental design determines the appropriate statistical testing procedure*, not the data that result from a study
12 - T
13 - F It is *not necessary for both groups to be the same size*; however, experiments are usually designed with equal samples sizes at the outset

Multiple Choice Questions

1 - D
2 - B
3 - C

Matching Terms

1 - c; 2 - g; 3 - i; 4 - h; 5 - j; 6 - k; 7 - f; 8 - b; 9 - e; 10 - d; 11 - a

Practice Problems

(1)

When s_1^2 is	N_1 is	s_2^2 is	and N_2 is	s_p^2 will be	and $s_{\bar{X}_1-\bar{X}_2}$ will be
10.26	10	7.42	10	8.84	1.33
25.31	24	30.08	22	27.59	1.55
101.42	36	85.13	30	94.04	2.40
0.57	12	0.76	12	0.66	0.33
48.69	19	45.11	24	46.68	2.10
2.01	8	3.50	7	2.70	0.85

(2)

When $\bar{X}_1$ is	N_1 is	$\bar{X}_2$ is	N_2 is	and s_p^2 is	t will be
10.21	12	11.58	12	8.06	-1.182
28.56	24	19.83	25	2.64	+18.801
0.98	36	0.24	34	0.64	+3.868
40.67	10	43.94	10	3.87	-3.717
101.25	14	95.72	12	13.24	+3.863
1.03	20	1.59	24	4.51	-0.871

(3)

When $\bar{X}_1$	$\bar{X}_2$	N is	and s^2 is	t will be
11.54	13.97	12	20.96	-1.839
25.62	22.28	25	63.18	+2.101
1.07	2.14	36	0.81	-7.133
51.48	49.36	10	6.49	+2.632
147.39	150.02	40	22.53	-3.504
7.26	5.59	20	2.37	+4.851

(4)

When H_0 is	α is	N_1 is	and N_2 is	t_{crit} will be
$\mu_1 = \mu_2$	.05	36	36	$\|2.000\|$
$\mu_D = 0$	.05	12	12	$\|2.201\|$
$\mu_1 = \mu_2$	.05	24	22	$\|2.021\|$
$\mu_D = 0$	.01	10	10	$\|3.250\|$
$\mu_1 = \mu_2$	.01	20	24	$\|2.704\|$
$\mu_D = 0$	.01	64	64	$\|2.660\|$

Chapter 12 - Analysis of Variance

True/False Questions

1 - F An analysis of variance will produce a significant result *if any pair of means*, in a set of means, *differ significantly* from each other
2 - T
3 - T
4 - T
5 - F A Tukey *HSD* test should be conducted *only when the initial F test is statistically significant*
6 - T
7 - T
8 - F The *dependent variable is assumed to be measured on either an interval or ratio scale*; no assumptions are made about the level of measurement for the independent variable
9 - T
10 - T
11 - T
12 - F A statistically significant value for the F statistic *indicates that at least two of the means differ significantly from each other*
13 - T
14 - T

Multiple Choice Questions

1 - A
2 - C
3 - D
4 - B
5 - B

Matching Terms

1 - b; 2 - j; 3 - e; 4 - l; 5 - i; 6 - a; 7 - h; 8 - c; 9 - k; 10 - d; 11 - g; 12 - f

Practice Problems

(1)

When N_{tot} is	and k is	df_B will be	df_W will be	and F_{crit} will be
36	4	3	32	2.92
54	3	2	51	3.23
60	6	5	54	2.45
100	5	4	95	2.53
72	3	2	69	3.15
64	4	3	60	2.76
90	6	5	84	2.37

(2)

When MS_W is	N is	k is	and df_W is	HSD will be
128.19	60	4	56	5.54
1.04	30	5	25	0.78
0.90	42	3	39	0.51
2235.33	21	3	18	37.25
9.48	27	3	24	2.09
72.75	40	4	36	5.19

(3)

When df_B is	df_W is	MS_W is	and N is	S will be
3	56	7.67	60	2.95
2	39	1.91	42	1.35
4	25	1034.76	30	61.71
3	24	98.47	28	15.94
2	36	156.25	39	12.63
3	76	49.13	80	6.38

Chapter 13 - Two-Way Analysis of Variance

True/False Questions

1 - F *The number of treatment groups is equal to a•b* which in this case is 4•3 = 12
2 - T
3 - T
4 - F *Interactions are bidirectional*; if factor *A* interacts with factor *B*, then factor *B* must interact with factor *A*.
5 - T
6 - F Generally, if the plot of a variable's *means are not parallel to the X axis there is some main effect for that variable*; the effect may or may not be significant in a statistical test
7 - T
8 - T
9 - F The secondary partitioning in a two-way ANOVA involves *the between-treatments sum of squares*
10 - T
11 - T
12 - F The size of the mean difference cannot be used to decide whether an effect is significant; *when N is small, even large differences may be due to chance factors*
13 - T

Multiple Choice Questions

1 - B A factorial design allows a researcher to evaluate the joint effects of two independent variables; this allows a researcher to determine if the effects of one independent variable "depend" on some second factor
2 - C
3 - B Because the lines are not parallel to each other there is an interaction effect; because the mean differences between the two age groups are different in each of the conditions there is also a main effect for unobserved/observed; because the average decision time for both of the age groups is about the same across the two conditions there is no main effect for age

Matching Terms

1 - h; 2 - g; 3 - a; 4 - f; 5 - b; 6 - c; 7 - e; 8 - d

Practice Problems

(1)

When N is	a is	and b is	df_A will be	df_B will be	df_{AxB} will be	and df_W will be
120	3	4	2	3	6	108
72	2	3	1	2	2	66
80	4	5	3	4	12	60
150	5	2	4	1	4	140

Chapter 14 - Repeated-Measures Analysis of Variance

True/False Questions

1 - T
2 - T
3 - F *Experimental error only includes random differences that result from procedural factors*, the random differences that occur due to naturally occurring individual *differences between research participants are referred to as sampling error*
4 - F If the error term were not partitioned into two separate components in a repeated-measures analysis the F statistic would *tend to be smaller*
5 - T
6 - T
7 - F Many research questions involving multiple conditions cannot be accurately tested using a repeated-measures design due to *potential carryover effects*
8 - F Within a given sample, the proportion of variation in the dependent variable explained by the independent variable manipulation is determined by calculating eta-squared (η^2).

Multiple Choice Questions

1 - D $df_{\text{subjects x treatment}} = (k - 1)(N - 1)$
2 - C
3 - B
4 - D

Matching Terms

1 - a; 2 - h; 3 - d; 4 - e; 5 - i; 6 - b; 7 - f; 8 - c; 9 - a

Practice Problems

(1)

When SS_{tot} is	$SS_{\text{between treatments}}$ is	and $SS_{\text{between subjects}}$ is	$SS_{\text{subjects x treatments}}$ is
4962	951	3600	411
512	112	295	105
98	34	51	13
3457	492	2847	118
946	82	618	246
2971	496	1489	986

(2)

When $SS_{\text{between treatments}}$ is	$SS_{\text{subjects x treatments}}$ is	k is	and N is	F will be
901	411	4	10	19.73
98	186	5	16	7.90
52	35	3	40	57.94
347	1104	3	24	7.23
1025	496	3	35	70.26
126	264	4	8	3.34

(3)

When $SS_{\text{subjects x treatments}}$ is	N is	and k is	HSD will be
126	12	4	2.17
15	8	5	1.08
63	20	3	1.00
2196	30	3	3.86
94	14	3	1.79
229	24	4	1.39

Chapter 15 - Nonparametric Tests

True/False Questions

1 - T
2 - F Nonparametric tests relax a number of the assumptions associated with parametric tests but they still *require that the data in the sample are independent of one another*
3 - F Nonparametric tests are *chiefly used to analyze data measured on either a nominal or interval scale*
4 - T
5 - T
6 - F For χ^2 tests the null hypothesis is rejected *when the calculated value of the test statistic exceeds the critical value*
7 - T
8 - F The *expected frequencies in each cell should be greater than or equal to 5*; there is no limitation based on the observed frequencies
9 - T
10 - T
11 - F The *Mann-Whitney U test does not use difference scores*; the Wilcoxen *T* test ignores difference scores of 0 when calculating the value for the test statistic
12 - F The value for T_{crit} is determined by the *total number of nonzero differences* in the data set
13 - T
14 - T

Multiple Choice Questions

1 - D
2 - D φ^2 is equal to χ^2/N
3 - B With a small number of matched pairs or repeated measures the Wilcoxen *T* is the most appropriate statistical test
4 - A There are two groups of subjects and 16 categories; $df = (r - 1)(c - 1) = 15$

Matching Terms

1 - f; 2 - h; 3 - k; 4 - a; 5 - c; 6 - j; 7 - b; 8 - g; 9 - d; 10 - e; 11 - i

Practice Problems

(1)

When the population proportion is	and N individuals are tested	the expected frequency count will be
0.15	400	60.00
0.72	60	43.20
0.33	40	13.20
0.49	32	15.68
0.02	81	1.62
0.65	144	93.60

(2)

When N_A is	N_B is	ΣR_A is	and ΣR_B is	U will be
8	4	36	42	0
9	6	81	39	18
10	8	69	102	14
6	9	62	58	13
4	10	40	65	10
7	7	71	34	6
15	12	126	252	6